Magnetic
ALLURE

Magnetic
ALLURE

The Blueprint to Building a Network of Referral Partners

MALIA ROGERS

Foreword by Michael McCormick

RADIANT LIGHT PUBLISHING INC.

Radiant Light Publishing
PO Box 2966
Hayden, ID 83835

www.MaliaRogers.com

ISBN (paperback): 979-8-9903917-0-3
ISBN (ebook): 979-8-9903917-1-0
ISBN (audio): 979-8-9903917-2-7

First paperback edition June 2024

Printed in the USA

This book is dedicated to:

My husband Chris, who inspires me and is
one of the most interesting people you'll ever meet.

My daughters Reaghan and Avalyn,
two of my greatest blessings in life.

And my Uncle Gary, who took a chance and sponsored
my immigrant parents to America, which forever
impacted the future generations in my family tree.

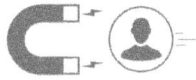

Contents

Foreword

BY MICHAEL MCCORMICK

In an era of inflation, rising lead costs, transient and transactional clients, and surface-level friendships, learning how to develop an army of people proactively sourcing and sending you business is a key to long-standing success in any industry. The quality of any lead from a trusted colleague and peer cannot be understated, as it arrives on your plate with the know, like, and trust factors that make it so much easier to earn a new client practically baked in.

Navigating the intricate world of insurance, where success hinges on the depth and breadth of one's professional network, Malia Rogers emerges within the industry as a pillar of relationship-building and strategic foresight. My acquaintance with Malia dates back to 2017. She has evolved from a client to a friend, and ultimately, I have been a beneficiary of her exceptional skills as a health insurance agent for myself and our employees across various enterprises. This rich tapestry of interaction and the various elements of our ever-evolving relationship have allowed me to have a deep knowledge of Malia both personally and professionally.

In my role as co-founder of the largest and most active community on Facebook for insurance agents, Insurance Soup™, which has over 50,000 members, my focus has been on fostering a vibrant community for insurance agents across the United States where agents who provide value and insight lead conversations that help build up agents where they are weak. Malia has always been a standout in our community both for her selfless nature in helping and adding value *and* for the obvious level of expertise she wields each time she contributes. Malia's adeptness at nurturing referral partnerships is unparalleled. Her five-step process is a master class in converting relationship-building from an art to a science, making her a sought-after speaker at our conference and a revered figure in the insurance community.

As someone who has stood in the dual roles of referral partner and client, I can vouch for the transformative power of her methods. Her approach goes beyond traditional networking, focusing on authenticity and strategic engagement and fostering trust that leads to continuous referrals. In a profession where lasting connections are often rare, Malia's strategies offer a blueprint for cultivating relationships that are both meaningful and beneficial.

This book is a must-read for professionals looking to elevate their career through strategic relationship-building. Malia's insights provide a clear path from the daily grind to a more effortless and rewarding professional journey. Her expertise, as showcased in our interactions and her broader impact on the Insurance Soup™ community, underscores the value of deep, strategic connections in our industry. I wholeheartedly recommend diving into this book and applying its lessons. Under Malia's guidance, you're not just learning to build a network: you're learning to enrich your professional life with lasting, fruitful relationships.

–Michael McCormick, co-founder of Insurance Soup™
and all Soup brands, conference host, industry investor,
speaker, and Insurtech advisory board member

Introduction

Cold calling, door knocking, and chasing leads is not fun for anyone in business. Many people think it's simply an essential part of growing your business from scratch. The good news is that there is an easier way to rapidly grow a business without subjecting yourself to getting punched in the gut with rejection day after day.

The question I'm asked most often by entrepreneurs is how I was able to quickly build a network of referral sources nationwide in a competitive industry. They wanted to know how I was able to thrive in an industry where statistically only 8 percent of people make it past their third year, without having to buy leads, cold call, or conduct meetings in person. Is there a magic formula? I wouldn't use that phrase, but something I have learned is the power of creating consistent and continuous referrals. I went from having my "office" at the foot of my bed (my husband had to sleep with the covers over his head when I stayed up late working), to building a successful team, an insurance agency, and mentoring other agents across the country in a relatively short amount of time. The biggest difference in how I built my business is that, instead of chasing prospects, they are hunting me down for help because someone they knew convinced them that I possess the solution to their problems.

My secret was to build "referral partners" or alliances with other people. These are other professionals who complement your business. There are several key reasons why this is essential to build your network of referral partners:

✧ 92 percent of consumers trust referrals from people they know. People are four times more likely to buy from you if they were referred (West, 2021).

✧ 84 percent of people prefer to find their service provider through a referral (Day, 2021).

✧ The average American is exposed to 4,000 to 10,000 ads per day.

✧ How do you stand out? When you're referred by someone they know, you will stand out.

✧ It's one of the few things you can do that will increase revenue and generate sales without increasing your marketing budget.

✧ It is a very effective way to spread your message. Instead of reaching out to one person at a time, you are leveraging another influencer's audience, who can spread your message to hundreds or thousands of people.

That favorable impression you make on one person can be exactly what pushes you to the next level. Early in my career, upon hearing what I was offering, one of my first referral partners said that I would need to hire an assistant because he was about to "blow up my business." I didn't believe him at the time, but he turned out to be telling the truth! Within a few months, I had to hire an assistant to keep up with the increase of incoming business.

By retracing my actions over the years, I developed a blueprint for building alliances and referral partners, which can be applied to almost any industry that relies on word-of-mouth marketing. I will explain my five-step process for building those key business relationships. However, one word of caution. After teaching these steps to hundreds of agents in my industry over the years, one of my biggest "aha moments" was realizing that going through these steps was not enough.

I previously held workshops and spoke at conferences on this very subject, but to my dismay, my "formula" worked for some agents, but not all. After brainstorming why that was, it finally occurred to me that you can't force others to do what you want. You can jump through all those steps, but if they don't want to send you business or work with you, they simply won't. I knew I had to figure out what makes someone want to send business to certain entrepreneurs, but not others. What is the "X factor?"

For example, according to the Department of Insurance in my home state of Idaho, they maintain over 114,000 insurance licenses, of which many are active agents I am competing with for business. The insurance industry is heavily regulated, so my competitor down the street is offering the same exact products and services as I am. Why would a financial advisor or a local doctor recommend me over my competitor? Now multiply my competition at a nationwide level; that is a lot of competition. I am also conducting business at a national level and I'm competing for business where I am unable to meet clients face-to-face. Why would anyone in a different state trust me enough to send their clients to me when they could just send their client to a local agent? My initial, honest self-assessment showed I was not necessarily more experienced or offering anything fancy that my competitors couldn't offer.

Still, I realized there was something that I had been doing since starting my entrepreneurship journey: self-improvement and character-building. That's why I concluded that while you can't force others to send you business, you can make changes to yourself. These changes will make you someone people want to meet and with whom they want to do business. Ever since I came to that conclusion, I have become obsessed with studying magnetic people and the science behind this strategy.

A magnet is material or an object that produces an invisible magnetic field that can attract other materials or objects. Have you ever met someone to whom you were powerfully drawn? People can be magnetic too!

I started paying attention to all the interesting people in my life. I read about and watched videos of people who have large numbers of followers and took notes on their behaviors and characteristics. The encouraging thing I found was what makes someone "attractive" has little to do with physical appearance, but rather characteristics that can be developed and built over time. Some of the people I've studied have even claimed they were once awkward and unpolished, which I found inspirational. So, the key to building referral partners that I previously missed when sharing my strategy with others is that you need to make yourself magnetic. This is as or even more important than following my five-step process to building referral partners; however, it is an ongoing process of improvement that could take time to master. Focusing on self-improvement will draw people to you. Other professionals will want to refer business to you and people will want to partner on business deals with you. This can also help you attract a larger pool of quality employees, which is a growing concern of business owners these days.

I believe that anyone can be magnetic! Now some of you may be thinking, "That's just not my personality," or, "I'm just not a vivacious person." However, did you know that even nonmetal objects can be magnetic if they have an electric charge? So, if an inanimate object can be magnetic, so can you, and I'm going to help you find that electric charge!

Among the challenges entrepreneurs face while building their business is fear of rejection and holding themselves accountable when they wake up and don't feel like "putting themselves out there." We will cover techniques and tricks to get over this fear and set yourself up for success.

Before we dive deeper into the strategies, allow me to share a personal journey. Once upon a time, I was a profoundly shy and reserved individual. The thought of speaking to strangers caused me anxiety and I would shrink from any opportunity to stand out, even when, as a student, it meant not raising my hand in class when I knew the answer. However, through efforts to push past my comfort zone and invest in self-character building, I have evolved from being that shy young girl to where I stand today. I hope you will consider my story as a reminder that we need not be confined by who we once were but instead embrace change and strive towards becoming the best versions of ourselves by understanding that we can undergo a transformation without sacrificing our authenticity.

By the time you are done reading this book, you should be able to implement strategies and techniques on how to:

✧ Identify your potential referral partners and alliances, how to approach them, and the dos and don'ts of your meetings with them

✧ Develop the art of building human connection and rapport, including building the "know, like, trust" factor

✧ Understand characteristics that make people attractive and how to develop them (including how to be an interesting person, be a better storyteller, engage people on social media, create a network or tribe of supporters, build charisma, and more)

✧ Set referral partner building goals and track your activity and progress

✧ Overcome the fear of rejection and hold yourself accountable

I hope you create waves in your industry and that your peers and competition start to take notice. I know you will experience a snowball effect on your business and an avalanche of clients coming to you for help at a rate that requires you to ramp up your staffing! Everyone has a unique set of experiences and skills that no one else in this world has. Let's unlock your full potential and apply these strategies to make you unstoppable!

The "Road Map"

Five Steps to Building Referral Partners

"Because the greatest part of a road trip isn't arriving at your destination. It's all the wild stuff that happens along the way."

–Emma Chase, author of *Tamed*

Have you ever been on an epic road trip? Your journey to building referral partners is much like going on a similar journey. Your passengers can make your trip either super fun or boring. The conversations you have, the landmarks you visit, and the roads you take can make the journey memorable or not. I'm going to give you a road map (more like a road guide) to plan your adventure, and it will be up to you to go as far as you would like to explore. You decide the radius of where your business will serve. Some will want to stick around and get to know their local area or home state well. Others may want to explore the nation or even be a world traveler. Here are those steps:

Step 1 starts with identifying where your ultimate destination will be, which in your journey as an entrepreneur may be to become well-known for serving your target market.

Not everyone is your ideal client. Who is your target market? What are your clients' demographics? Are they business owners, a certain age group, have certain interests, within a specific income range? Do they own certain assets and work in specific occupations or industries? Do they have certain spending habits or a specific life event, life goals, or a specific need or problem that your services or product will resolve? Make a list of characteristics of your ideal client and create a "profile" for them so you can easily identify who you want to serve. The more specifically you can narrow down and identify who your ideal client is, the easier it will be to identify where to find them.

Step 2 identifies who you want to join you for the ride.

Who are your potential referral partners and who do your ideal clients buy from before they buy from you? Your best bet would be to choose someone who owns a business that complements your market, while ideally having similar target markets. Picture your ideal clients (from Step 1) going through a chain of events . . . what kinds of problems do they run into before needing your services, and who do they turn to for help resolving those issues? After making a list of ideal clients, list next to each demographic who is already providing solutions to that group.

For example, if you are a real estate agent, you are looking for people who are ready to buy and sell properties. Naturally, buyers will be working with mortgage loan officers to qualify for a loan. Loan officers understand that real estate agents can be a strong source of referrals since people shopping for real estate may potentially need to secure a loan to make their purchase. Therefore, real estate agents and loan officers are considered "power referral partners" with tons of opportunities to send business to each other.

Some professional referral resources may be obvious, but many sources may not be as obvious. For example, if you owned an alarm security business, you may already know that home and auto insurance agents are consistently asking clients if they own a security system in their homes (which can affect their insurance rates). If the insurance agent followed up each time the response was "no" with a question that uncovers interest in adding security to their home, they could drum up business for you. See Appendix A for a list of top careers that rely on referrals and their top referral partners' ideas.

Surprisingly, I learned that one of my strongest referral partners turned out to be my competitor, so don't rule them out! Collaborating with your competitors can create an increase in business for both of you. Do you provide services that your competitors do not, and vice versa? In the insurance industry, some agents only specialize in specific markets. Insurance agents who only sell home and auto insurance can refer clients to agents (such as myself) who specialize in Medicare or health insurance, and vice versa. Make a list of the type of professionals you would like to connect with, who you personally know that fit those profiles, and how you can connect with them.

Step 3 is where you explore the possibility of inviting your potential referral partners on the journey with you. Reach out to them individually to schedule a one-on-one to get to know them. Keep in mind that this is not a sales call, and you are not selling anything to them at this point. You are inviting them to brainstorm and possibly partner in building each other's businesses together.

When you approach your potential referral partner, you are simply going to introduce yourself, tell them who you are, what you do, and why you would like to meet with them. You could say something along the lines of, "I'm a (insert your occupation) and sometimes run into people who need (insert your potential referral partner's service). Can we get together for coffee or lunch so I can learn more about what you have to offer my clients and maybe collaborate?"

This does not necessarily need to be face-to-face. I have never met most of my referral partners, and I'm embarrassed to admit that I do not even know what some of them look like because we have only spoken over the phone.

Do not try to solicit them for business in this step; you truly need time set aside to learn about this person (during your "one-on-one" in Step 4) to figure out whether they would be someone you would want "riding" with you. Asking them to join you (or send you business) before you have had a chance to get to know each other or vetting them is the equivalent of asking a total stranger to go on a road trip with you. You will seem desperate, aggressive, and the chances of them saying yes to you (no matter how cool you are) will be much lower than if they already know you.

Step 4 is where you get to know your potential new referral partner, and vice versa, to decide if you could possibly take that road trip together. There are key elements for a successful one-on-one connection with your potential referral partner. Get to know them by asking questions, and make sure you don't talk about yourself the entire time! Keep in mind, as humans, generally the more we think someone knows about us, the more we like them.

One of my best friends, Jacquie Walter (who is a brilliant entrepreneur and broker, also in the insurance industry), introduced me to the "Traffic Light Rule," often used as a guideline in conversations to ensure everyone in the conversation has a chance to participate and prevents any one person from dominating the discussion. Marty Nemko, career coach, author, and radio host, illustrates this rule: "During the first thirty seconds of an utterance, your light is green, in the second thirty it's yellow, and after sixty seconds, the benefits of continuing to talk usually are outweighed by the advantages of shutting up or asking a question. If the person wants to know more, they can ask—they rarely will. Think of a conversation as a ping-pong game: the ball goes quickly from side to side."

The first goal during this meeting is to vet them so that you can gauge how trustworthy they are. You're not going to send your clients to just anyone! The second goal is to learn how to send them business. If you've ever been a part of a business networking group, they talk about their "GAINS," which stands for goals, accomplishments, interests, networks, and skills. Make sure you learn their GAINS and that they know yours as well.

Before the end of your one-on-one, you must extract "trigger phrases" from them and give them "trigger phrases" in return. What are some of the phrases they might hear from your ideal clients that would cue them to start the referral process? These phrases seem obvious to you as the industry pro but may not be for someone not in your line of work. For example, as a health insurance agent, I would need to teach my potential referral partner that when someone leaves or loses their job, that person would most likely need help with securing their own health insurance, which would hopefully prompt my partner to make an introduction to me. Get good at listening so that you can be better at referring business!

Step 5 is all about tracking your progress and goals. When I started intentionally building referral partners, my goal was to add one new referral partner each month. It is a numbers game, so you need to break down monthly, weekly, and daily activity goals. If you reach out to two potential partners per day, it should result in three to five one-on-ones per week, which will lead you to one new solid referral partner a month. You can double or triple the activity for greater results. You can download a free workbook that includes a daily activity tracker at: **www.MaliaRogers.com**. Always ask new prospects how they heard about you. This is how you know who's riding along in your journey with you and who hasn't gotten into the vehicle with you yet. Track your referrals through your customer relationship management software (CRM). Some of you may be using a simple spreadsheet, which is okay, as long as you are tracking!

It does not matter where you are going, it's who's riding along with you. Not everyone will want to ride along with you, and to have your pick of traveling companions, or to convince someone to ride along with you, you need to be magnetic! The next nine chapters of this book will go over each characteristic that magnetic people have and how to develop these characteristics over time, which will be essential to building referral partners. I encourage you to start practicing these five steps while allowing yourself time to build those magnetic characteristics. It's important not to fall into the trap of waiting until you feel you've perfected these characteristics before reaching out to potential referral partners. Start the five steps sooner rather than later, even as you continue to refine your magnetism.

Chapter 1 Smart Moves

1. List and describe your ideal client.

2. Next to each demographic from your ideal client list, identify and list your potential referral partners.

3. Reach out to your potential referral partners and invite them to meet with you for a one-on-one.

4. Conduct your one-on-ones. Get to know them, vet them, and learn how to refer business to them.

5. Download the free workbook that includes a daily activity tracker at: www.MaliaRogers.com

    Set and track your goals and activity.

CHAPTER 2

Magnetic Allure
—Unleashing the Interesting Person from Within
Why and how to be an interesting person

"Interesting people are interested in things other than themselves."

–Jessica Hagy, Author

Why should you be interesting? My friend Gaylan Hendricks, an insurance industry titan, has always reminded us that "people aren't going to be interested unless you are interesting." What makes a person interesting? Someone that is interesting keeps your attention because he or she is unusual, exciting, or has a lot of ideas.

When I had the idea to write this book, I started observing the interesting people in my life. My husband is the closest person in my life who is interesting, so I noted his habits to try to pinpoint what it was that made him intriguing. After observing his behavior and habits, it occurred to me that there are three key elements that make a person interesting or intriguing to others:

1. Interesting people have the ability to get hyper-focused, obsessed, or fully immerse themselves in a particular topic or subject. To "geek out," or be passionate, instead of just dabbling in a particular subject. For example: my husband was given the opportunity to raise bees a couple of years ago. In a very short period, he watched and read hundreds of videos and articles and befriended beekeepers to find out what it takes to care for bees. For a while, I would be having a full-on conversation with him and could tell he was beekeeping in his head. For the first time in his life, he noticed spring flowers in bloom because that meant more pollen for his bees to collect. He even studied what beekeepers did in Russia to give their bees the best chance for survival in extreme weather.

He has also started a "beard collection," collecting selfies with random bearded strangers, now has hundreds of photos in his collection and started an Instagram, as well as YouTube Channel called, "Beard Meets Beard!"

The key is to feed your mind and to develop unique perspectives by reading articles, watching videos, listening to podcasts about interesting topics, and studying interesting people. Do a search on Facebook for groups that have the word "interesting" in their name and join to share and read interesting things (look for groups with large amounts of members and more frequent posts per week). Develop an interest or curiosity in other people and their life stories. Interview the interesting people in your life to expand your perception of life. "Being with someone interesting automatically makes *you* more interesting—not just by association, but because you collect more interesting material to pass on" (Busch, 2023).

2. The second element of becoming known as an interesting person is being comfortable with showing your authentic self and being genuine. What does it mean to be authentic and genuine, and what are the differences? Being authentic means you are being true to yourself, you are comfortable in your own skin, and you are not seeking the approval of others, even when things you are interested in are not mainstream. Authentic items are often described as "original, not imitated," which is crucial to the perceived value of the item. Humans are the same. We each have our unique talents and life experiences, so if we can showcase our true selves, we will be regarded as having more value.

Being genuine relates to how others relate to you. What they see is what they get; you don't have hidden agendas and people view you as trustworthy and reliable. "Most of us have an innate sixth sense for insincerity. When we feel like someone is hiding who they really are, we tend to see it a mile off. People who put on a front we usually interpret as being disingenuous. We can see they are not being themselves and so we have a harder time trusting them" (Jackson, 2023).

3. The third element, which is equally important, is sharing your interests with the world. You can be the most interesting person out there, but if you don't ever share your knowledge with others, no one will know you are an interesting person. Share facts and interesting info you have learned either by working it into conversations, sharing on social media, or creating and sharing videos about your topic to demonstrate your expertise.

My friend Melissa Dillon, known as "The Insurance Exam Queen," exemplifies what can happen when you embody these elements. Melissa is incredibly passionate about teaching people how to pass their insurance exams. In 2022, she began uploading videos filled with memory tricks and quips to help people retain the necessary information to pass their exams. She is unapologetically herself, not seeking approval from others. Melissa doesn't care if you don't like her rainbow mohawk (she really rocks that hair style though), and the fun facial expressions on her YouTube thumbnails are captivating. As of 2024, just two years later, she has nearly forty-three thousand subscribers and has made millions by sharing her passion while helping others achieve their professional goals.

If you feel you don't have time to start a new hobby or you don't feel like an interesting person, you can share the interesting things your spouse, kids, friends, or loved ones are involved in.

Being an interesting person can also mean making interesting choices. Interesting people can come up with interesting solutions when faced with tough situations. On January 15, 2009, a US Airways plane struck a flock of large birds shortly after takeoff from New York City, causing a loss of engine power. The plane's pilots, Chelsey "Sully" Sullenberger and Jeffrey Skiles, decided to glide the plane and perform an emergency landing on the Hudson River off Manhattan. All 155 passengers survived, and the media dubbed this water landing "the Miracle on the Hudson," which made aviation history. This was such an interesting decision that it inspired the film *Sully* to share this story in 2016, with Tom Hanks portraying Sullenberger.

Interesting people have also made interesting mistakes. John Leonard was the twenty-one-year-old college student who became famous for coming up with a loophole in a promotion to obtain enough Pepsi Points to earn a jet through a sweepstake. In the mid-1990s, PepsiCo launched a marketing campaign where customers could collect points to claim prizes. One commercial advertised a Harrier Jet for seven million points, and there were no disclaimers indicating it was a joke. Leonard figured out he could purchase points and calculated the $32 million jet could technically be purchased for only $700,000, so he convinced five investors to help him purchase those points. His journey was so interesting that Netflix ran a docuseries entitled *Pepsi, Where's My Jet?*

Do something unique! My friend, Teresa Ferrin, a health broker out of Arizona, was volunteering at a thrift store. One day she found a Purple Heart War medal and proceeded to do her own investigation to find the rightful owner, who was all the way across the country. It took weeks for her to track down the war hero's next of kin, but she didn't give up. She successfully delivered the war medal into the right hands. This was such a moving and unique story, she ended up being featured by nationally recognized media outlets such as ABC's *Good Morning America*, and even *People* magazine reached out to interview her.

Another way to become interesting is to practice curiosity and inquisitiveness. Those little kids who always asked "why this or that" to everything most likely have become interesting adults. Keep in mind, you can't be interesting as a follower, so take the road less traveled and choose hobbies or topics you are passionate about, even if they are not mainstream.

If you cultivate a life that is interesting, you are willing to share your unique perspective with the world. If you are passionate and genuine, people will find you interesting. Here is a final question to ask yourself: if a movie were to be made about your year, what would the title be, and would it be interesting?

Becoming known as an interesting person holds value in building referral partnerships. By finding your unique passions, embracing authenticity, and sharing your knowledge with others, you will not only captivate others but also lay the foundation for building connections.

Chapter 2 Smart Moves

1. Make a list of your hobbies and figure out which topic generates the most queries on a search engine.

2. Interview someone interesting in your life. (Bonus points if you record and share clips of your interview.

3. Make a daily goal of feeding your mind (either by reading, watching, or listening) and track your activity.

4. Share something interesting about your hobby, something you learned, or someone you found interesting at least two times a week on any social media platform and track your activity.

CHAPTER 3

The Tribe Attraction —Magnetize Your Meaningful Connections
Why and How to Find Your People

"Be around the light bringers, the magic makers, the world shifters, the game shakers. They challenge you, break you open, uplift and expand you. They don't let you play small with your life. These heartbeats are your people. These people are your tribe."

— Danielle Doby, Author

Magnetic people always have a tribe backing them up. What is a tribe and why should you have one? Your tribe is made of people with whom you surround yourself. They have your back, accept you for who you are, cheer you on when you are winning, lift you up when you are going through a rough patch, encourage, inspire, and push you to become the best version of you.

Humans are created for connection, and according to Maslow's hierarchy of needs, after food and safety, the next most important need is the sense of belonging or acceptance. Did you know that who you spend the most time with can influence or shape your future? Jim Rohn, a motivational speaker, suggested that we are the average of the five people we spend the most time with. That's why you must choose the people for your tribe wisely! If your friends are volunteering and serving the community, you are more likely to serve as well. If your friends are creating and posting content on YouTube, you will be more likely to start a YouTube channel. If most of your friends are writing and publishing books, then you will be more likely to publish a book.

Another benefit to having a tribe is that while it's tacky to brag about yourself, if you have people who believe in you and they are quick to point out your skills and talents, you gain instant clout with whatever you are trying to accomplish. People are more likely to believe what others are saying about you, rather than what you say about yourself. This is why word-of-mouth marketing is so effective! We will discuss the importance of collecting client testimonials later in this book, but as for your tribe . . . not only is it important to have this support system through your entrepreneurial journey of ups and downs, but having a tribe can create a "PayPal Mafia" effect.

The "PayPal Mafia" is a tight-knit group of former PayPal employees who went on to create successful multibillion-dollar companies that have become household names such as Tesla, SpaceX, LinkedIn, YouTube, Yelp, Yahoo!, and many more. Not only was this particular group filled with intellectually curious, entrepreneurial, and bright mindsets, but they also used the power of networking. They had contacts in the right places to help each other launch their billion-dollar ideas. They amplified, supported, invested in, and vouched for each other's businesses.

How do you find your tribe? It's true that "your vibe attracts your tribe." You are what you attract. The first step is to make a list of all the traits of your ideal "bestie." Is this person generous, kind, ambitious, funny, intellectual, have integrity, empathetic, a good listener, and confident? Next, ask yourself if you embody these traits. People who have integrity hang out with others who also have integrity. People who have positive mindsets won't want to spend time with people who have negative attitudes. Work on yourself and the characteristics you find attractive for friends to have and people with similar traits will be naturally drawn to you. You will want to conduct a tribe audit. Evaluate who you are spending the most time with and determine if these people have traits you value in friendship. Who are the five people with whom you spend the most time? You can only find your tribe if you put yourself out there and get involved.

As you work on nurturing qualities within yourself that align with your ideal "tribe," it's crucial to actively engage with communities and opportunities. Did you ever play with magnets when you were a kid? Remember when you took a magnet and held it to various objects to see what sticks? Finding your tribe is the same thing. Discovering your tribe involves exploring various avenues and being open to different experiences.

Join networking groups or other groups that have something in common with an activity or interest you are passionate about. Put yourself out there and be visible. Don't just attend networking meetings, get involved with what the group is doing and get to know the members. I learned a tip from my friend Becky Rill, who is a master networker. She shared a strategy to use at a networking event, especially if you are going solo. Look for groups of odd-numbered people to join. Groups with an even number of people, especially pairs, can often be more closed off in their conversations. They may be deeply immersed in a one-on-one discussion, making it harder for an outsider to break in and join the conversation naturally. In a group of three, it's common for one person to feel slightly left out or be less engaged in the conversation. This creates a natural opening for a fourth person to join the group. The person feeling left out will often be more welcoming to another participant, making it easier for you to integrate.

Before jumping into a group, observe from a distance. Look for body language cues. Are they standing in a closed circle or are there gaps? Are they all actively engaged, or does someone look like they're scanning the room or not fully engrossed in the discussion? Once you've chosen a group, approach it with confidence. Remember, networking events are designed for mingling and meeting new people. Once you've joined a group, listen for a moment before jumping in. This allows you to understand the topic at hand and contribute meaningfully. Once you're in the conversation, try to engage everyone in the group. You truly get what you put in. If you simply show up and leave right after the meetings, you don't get the time to get to know others and vice versa.

If the group is volunteering to support a greater cause, roll up your sleeves and show up to help. If someone in the group is recovering from surgery, offer to set up a meal train. People will remember what you did for them when they needed help more often than you will remember what you did for them. Now, you may be wondering, why am I suggesting you do all this community service and help people you don't know very well? When you help others, you end up intrinsically benefiting more than you realize. Did you know the quickest way to get out of a funk is to focus on others' needs?

Surprisingly, social media is one of the best places to find your tribe. (For more on social media, read Chapter 9.) There are three useful ways to find your tribe on social media:

1. Posting about things that interest you will naturally draw people that resonate with you, who would be drawn to you.

2. Reach out and befriend people . . . you can do searches on topics that interest you through social media platforms. If you are into fitness or love to travel, and you see a post that resonates with you, reach out to the person who posted and explain what you liked about the post. Invite someone to coffee or have a Zoom conversation. It might feel strange at first to approach someone you don't know, but if you lead with value, he or she will more likely be open for friendship with you. Some of my favorite people I met over social media have become like family, and it is empowering for you to be able to handpick your tribe from all over the world.

3. Facebook groups allow you to connect with people who share common interests. I have met so many friends in my industry from all over the country this way. You know what's better than meeting besties from a Facebook group? Creating and growing one yourself!

My friends Michael McCormick and Taylor Dobbie had an idea to create an environment where insurance agents can discuss anything related to the industry, and in just a very short time they grew the Insurance Soup™ Facebook group to over 53,000 members (as of 2024). This is where I give much credit to my business success: from the relationships I have built through this group. They maintained engagement and built traction by teaching marketing skills and business strategies to their members. They post things in the group that motivate, inspire, and make us laugh. Many members have described the group as having a family vibe, and so many friendships were created through this group, they finally started hosting conferences (Soup Live) for members to unite, meet face-to-face, learn, and grow together. It has become one of the most anticipated events for members in the group.

My friend Jason Hamilton, a certified financial planner, is the founder of "Your Retirement Coach," a thriving Facebook community that covers all topics related to the questions people want to know about retirement planning. His group has flourished and rapidly grown to over 30,000 members. His success is no accident: Jason consistently hosts informative workshops for members in the group, invites other professionals such as myself as resources for his group, and uploads tons of educational materials into the group files for the members of his group.

Your Facebook group does not have to be industry-related. My friend Keith Boe, an award winning real estate agent, created several successful Facebook groups: "North Idaho Life," which covers the beauty and happenings of our local area; "North Idaho Cuisine," highlighting local eateries; "North Idaho Life Snow Angels," a group where complete strangers volunteer or ask for help with snow removal for the elderly or disabled members of the community; and a few other groups as well. Combined members in all his groups total over 200,000, which makes him somewhat of a celebrity in his community. He says, "A Facebook group is a reflection of its owner(s): their values, enjoyment, personality, and heart. Post only what you truly love with no agenda and your tribe will find you. If you love cats, share all your cat love, anecdotes, and cool finds. The cat people will find you."

The key to building these groups is to create value, centered around the topic of your group. People start to feel like they know you, start regarding you as an "expert" or an authority figure and they will naturally want to support your business and personal endeavors. You will notice higher social media engagement with people who have built their tribe this way. This takes time and patience to build, but not only can you create a tribe and business relationships that will generate clients for your business through this endeavor, but it may also open doors for other sources of revenue. Notice that the examples of creating or finding your tribe involves providing some sort of service or giving back to others. Service to others is a huge part of being magnetic. Chapter 7 will discuss this topic in detail. The best leaders serve others, so it's essential to be willing to use your God-given talents to bless others. The other important but basic factor in finding your tribe is to show up. Just show up. Show up, even when you sometimes don't feel like it.

Building a supportive tribe is essential for cultivating lasting referral partnerships. Your tribe not only provides encouragement but also serves as a network of like-minded individuals who can amplify your endeavors. So, invest in meaningful connections and watch your tribe become a cornerstone of your professional journey!

Chapter 3 Smart Moves

1. List the traits of your ideal best friend, evaluate where you embody those traits, and complete a "tribe audit"

2. Research or list all the networking groups that you would be interested in joining:

    a. Attend meetups to get a feel for the group's "culture" to decide if they would be a good fit or "vibe."

    b. Connect with a few potential referral partners and ask for one-on-ones, using the five steps in Chapter 1 of this book.

    c. Get involved in your group's community services and or socials.

3. Think of subjects in which you are knowledgeable or passionate about for which you can create a Facebook community around:

    a. Think of and list all the possible group names for your group. Research if the name is already taken. It's OK to create a new group surrounding a topic for which a group already exists.

    b. Create the group and invite friends to join and invite their friends to join.

    c. Post engaging content that engages members in the group.

CHAPTER 4

Cultivating Your "Magnetic Signature Voice"

Why the Sound of Your Voice Matters and Elements that Reflect Your Personal Brand

"There are four ways, and only four ways, in which we have contact with the world. We are evaluated and classified by these four contacts: what we do, how we look, what we say, and how we say it."

— Dale Carnegie, Writer and Speaker

I had a funny conversation with a prospect recently. Towards the end of our phone call, she mentioned that judging from my headshot, she was expecting to hear from someone with a higher pitched, softer, more childlike voice. She was pleasantly surprised that my voice was low and deep. Upon hearing the sound of my voice, she jokingly thought to herself, "Yessss, take my money and tell me what to do with it!" One time, she said, she was getting to know a man she met on an online dating site and was super excited and hopeful . . . but then when they finally met, the sound of his voice ruined it for her.

Have you ever met someone in person who didn't look like how you pictured him or her when you spoke over the phone? Has something similar ever happened to you? Why do you think this happens? It's because we subconsciously make judgments about people, based on the sound of their voice. Yes, the sound of your voice can influence how people view you. I recently volunteered to judge at a National Christian Forensics and Communications Association (NCFCA) Speech and Debate League tournament and let me tell you, within the first three seconds of people's speech, it was difficult not to make judgments on whether their speech was going to be good or not. Your voice has the power to capture and hold your audience's attention, which can make you magnetic.

Our individual voice is a remarkably unique aspect of our identity, as distinct as our fingerprint that sets us apart from others. Our voice is like a musical instrument, so it makes sense to learn how to harness the power and sound to discover your signature voice. Here are some key elements of an appealing voice:

1. **Tone:** Use an appropriate tone that conveys the emotion or intention behind your message. A well-modulated tone can make your speech easier to listen to and more engaging. According to a scientific study at UCLA, your words only account for about 7 percent of your credibility, or whether people like you and think you're smart, funny, strong, or successful. By contrast, tonality—the sounds your voice makes aside from the words—counts for more than 38 percent. (See, Love, n.d.) A deeper, richer vocal tone will command more respect and be viewed more authoritative.

2. **Pitch and Inflection:** A balanced pitch is essential for a pleasant speaking voice. Avoid speaking in a monotone or in an overly high or low pitch, as it can be challenging for listeners to engage with. Our vocal cords are like a musical instrument; according to studies, most people only talk in two notes while speaking. The same exact phrase can have a different meaning just by whether you take the phrase up or down the stairstep melody. Ascending melodies (a change in pitch from lower to higher note) make people happy, indicate questioning, surprise, or suspense. Avoid this while stating facts or closing a deal, or it could indicate uncertainty. Descending melodies (a change in pitch going from a higher to a lower note) can turn a phrase into a more serious or powerful statement, which would indicate confidence, power, and certainty.

3. **Volume:** Adjust your volume based on the setting and audience size. Speak loudly enough to be heard, but not so loud as to be overpowering or aggressive. The ideal volume is situational and requires you to be aware of and adapt to the context. In a larger room or if you are addressing a sizable group, you may need to project your voice more, while in a more intimate or one-on-one setting, a softer volume is more appropriate. If your message is meant to convey urgency or excitement, a slightly higher volume would be suitable, versus what you would use when discussing sensitive or confidential information. Depending on the context of what is being said, a higher volume can indicate several things: confidence, enthusiasm, dominance, agitation, or anger. There is also a range of what softer vocal volume can indicate: shyness, intimacy, calmness, politeness, or insecurity. Striking a balance between being too loud or too soft is essential

for effective communication. Be aware of your volume, think of your intentions and what you want to convey to your audience or to whom you're speaking. Observe your audience's reactions to ensure your level of volume is comfortable and effective.

4. **Pace:** Speak at a comfortable pace that allows your audience to follow along and absorb your message. Avoid speaking too quickly or too slowly, as both can hinder comprehension. Speaking quickly can convey excitement or enthusiasm; however, it can also make you seem nervous or impatient. Slow speech can convey calmness or thoughtfulness but can also make you appear lacking confidence or show disengagement. You can vary your pace, depending on the content and your audience's needs. Speak more slowly when conveying complex ideas, speed up slightly when covering straightforward information, and use pauses strategically to allow your audience to absorb the information and process your ideas. Pauses can create emphasis, while allowing you time to gather your thoughts, so don't be afraid of that brief silence! If you are about to speak in front of a large audience or have an important presentation, practice proper breathing techniques (which can be found on YouTube), focus on taking deep controlled breaths, and try to stay relaxed, as anxiety can cause you to speed up unintentionally.

Paying attention to your listeners' nonverbal cues, such as eye contact, facial expressions, and body language can help you adjust the various elements of your vocal sound. If all this information seems overwhelming, start by conducting a "voice audit." Record yourself speaking in different situations and listen to the playback. Analyze your tone, pitch, volume, pace, and inflection, and identify areas that need improvement. Are you nasally? Are you monotone? Do you sound too "airy," which can sometimes come off as fake? Look up YouTube videos on vocal exercise to improve the areas in which you're dissatisfied. Find a few different favorite vocal warmups on YouTube. Create and save them in a "vocal warmups playlist" for quick access so you can perform these frequently, such as while getting ready for your day or while you are driving or stuck in traffic. One of my favorite vocal coaches to follow on YouTube is Cheryl Porter. She has worked with famous artists, is one of the most sought-after vocal coaches in the world, has over seven million subscribers, and has developed her own vocal training method, which includes her own innovative approaches.

If public speaking is an important part of your professional life, I recommend hiring a one-on-one vocal coach for several reasons. You get customized instruction, tailored to your needs and goals. They can work with you to identify areas where you need improvement and develop a plan to help you achieve your goals. You also receive real-time feedback on your vocal sound, help you to identify areas where you need improvement, and adjust your technique accordingly. Also, when you have a vocal coach, you have someone holding you accountable and keeping you on track with your practice and progress.

At the beginning of the year, I started to publish insurance-related YouTube Videos for my clients and prospects. On an unrelated goal, in February, I decided to take singing lessons, as I have always wanted to take lessons and finally made the time to do so. Astonishingly, I have noticed a drastic improvement in tone and richness of my voice from my first YouTube videos, compared to my vocal tone in my videos just a couple of months after starting vocal lessons! I asked my vocal coach, Heather Erickson, about this and her research backed up why singing can improve your speech and vocal sound. She found that regular singing can expand the lung capacity and vocal range, which in turn generates a full and rich voice, capable of captivating the audience's attention. The trained vocalist will use their diaphragm for vocal power, instead of their throat. So, if you don't like the sound of your voice, try hiring a vocal coach or take singing lessons and practice, ideally in front of a mirror.

Heather suggested downloading a mobile app, called "Sing Sharp," which is designed to help people improve their singing voice, using a variety of tools and exercises including warm-ups, scales, and popular songs that users can practice singing along with (karaoke style). One of the features of "Sing Sharp" is its pitch-tracking technology. The app listens to the user's voice as he or she sings and provides real-time feedback on their pitch accuracy. This feedback can be visualized in the form of a pitch graph, which shows the user how close he or she is to hitting the correct pitch.

You can study speakers with appealing vocal tones and try to imitate their style. Analyze their breathing, pitch, and inflection patterns to understand how they achieve their desired tone. Observe and emulate your favorite speakers, to model their approach in your own performance.

Seek constructive feedback from trusted friends, colleagues, and mentors. While it may be intimidating to ask your peers for input and spotlight your voice, regular feedback can help you recognize areas for improvement and help you track your progress.

It's incredible how the sound of your voice can shape your image and how others perceive you. Remember that harnessing your vocal tone and finding your signature voice is a gradual process. Be patient and continue to consistently practice, developing a tone that is engaging, confident, and uniquely yours.

Discovering and refining your signature voice is a pivotal step in building referral partnerships. Your voice holds power in shaping perceptions and engaging audiences. By mastering elements such as your tone and pitch, you can captivate listeners and establish credibility. Invest in and embrace the journey of finding your signature voice, which will elevate your communication skills and foster meaningful connections with referral partners.

Chapter 4 Smart Moves

1. Record yourself speaking for one minute in various situations and conduct a voice audit.

2. Create a YouTube playlist of a variety of your favorite vocal warm-ups.

3. Schedule and perform daily or weekly vocal warm-ups on your calendar.

4. Enroll in singing lessons or download the free "Sing Sharp" app.

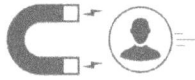

CHAPTER 5

Magnetic Insight–Unveiling Hidden Gems in Others

How to Be a "Talent Whisperer" and Recognize Potential in Others

"Believe in people and they will believe in themselves. Encourage their dreams, and they will be forever grateful, for you have watered the seeds of their potential."

— Unknown

Behind all great people is the support and belief of someone who saw their potential, even when they may not have seen it themselves. Take a moment to think of a person who saw potential in you, someone who believed in your abilities and encouraged you to chase your dreams. Think of that feeling of appreciation and warmth as you recall the moments of encouragement that propelled you forward. That is what draws people to magnetic people, who are often skilled at reading people, which enables them to identify unique qualities and potential that others may overlook. Don't underestimate the impact your encouragement can make on someone's life.

Someone did that for me a few years ago, which planted a seed in my head that opened doors for me, simply from my believing what he said to be true. In 2019, a mentor, a friend in the insurance industry, Michael McCormick from Insurance Soup™, pointed out something to me. Just one sentence. He had suggested that I would make a great speaker when someone in his Facebook group had asked for recommendations on speakers for an upcoming conference. This surprised me because at that point in my life, I had never done live videos, never been interviewed on a podcast, and my introverted self would be terrified at the thought of speaking in front of a large live audience. I was raised in a culture where there is an emphasis on respect for elders and children were expected to listen more while speaking less, so I remember not even being comfortable speaking to strangers until after I graduated from high school. However, after my friend planted that seed, I slowly grew more comfortable speaking in public. I've now spoken at several conferences; in fact, the first big stage was given to me by Michael and his business partner, Taylor Dobbie. I have been invited to share my knowledge on podcasts, have been featured in articles by nationally recognized brands, and even launched my YouTube channel! This was not a fluke, as Michael has done this for countless other individuals, including those I personally know as well.

Magnetic people can spot talent in others because of their strong interpersonal skills, which helps them connect with people on a deeper level. They can identify unique qualities and potential that others may overlook. They naturally make others feel valued and appreciated, which encourages individuals to share their skills, interests, and aspirations. Recognizing talent before the person sees it in themselves is also a leadership quality that makes people loyal to you.

How do you build that skill of unveiling talent in others? First, view people as a "10" and believe in them. It's easy to believe in people after they've become achievers, but it takes aptitude to see it in others before their skills have been developed. People rise to your expectations. Have you ever been around someone you feel thinks highly of you? You don't want to let that person down and you raise your game when around him or her.

This phenomenon can be explained by the "Rosenthal Effect," a psychological theory that suggests our expectations of a person can influence their performance. This effect was studied by Robert Rosenthal and Lenore Jacobson in the 1960s. They conducted an experiment in an elementary school, where they gave students a disguised IQ test at the start of the school year. They informed teachers that some of the students (selected at random and hence referred to as "bloomers") were expected to have an intellectual growth spurt during the year, when in reality, these children were no different from the others. At the end of the year, Rosenthal and Jacobson retested the students' IQs and found that the students labeled as "bloomers" improved their IQ scores significantly more than the other students. The only difference was the teachers' expectations, suggesting that these expectations had influenced the students' performances. Perhaps in this case, if a teacher believes that certain students are more intellectually gifted, they might unknowingly give those students more attention or encourage-ment, leading those students to perform better. This is a type of self-fulfilling prophecy, which is a prediction that causes itself to come true, due to the simple fact the prediction was made. So, the initial belief or expectation you may have of those around you may influence their behavior in a way that causes the expectation to be fulfilled.

Observe and look for these traits and qualities in those around you. You can look for the following characteristics to spot potential talent and help people reach their full potential:

1. **Passion:** Passion, curiosity, and genuine enthusiasm about their work or interests. Passionate and curious individuals are more likely to invest time and effort into developing their skills.

2. **Commitment:** How committed the person is to their work, whether they take responsibility for their tasks and follow through. A strong work ethic is often indicative of potential talent.

3. **Creativity:** The ability to think outside the box and come up with innovative solutions and problem-solving skills: people who are good at analyzing situations, identifying issues, and working on how to overcome them.

4. **Adaptability:** Being able to adapt to new situations and learn from experiences, someone open to change, who can quickly adjust to new environments or challenges.

5. **People Skills:** Interpersonal skills and the ability to work well in teams, as they often signify self-awareness. The ability to navigate complex social situations, build strong relationships, and respond appropriately to challenges.

6. **Initiative and Proactiveness:** Taking on responsibilities or seeking new opportunities. People with these traits often have great potential to grow and excel in their chosen fields.

7. **Track Record:** While past performance is not always a perfect indicator of future potential, it can provide valuable insight into a person's abilities and achievements.

Once you have spotted potential in someone, encourage that person! Your belief in their potential can help their self-confidence, allowing them to step out of their comfort zone to pursue their goals. It can inspire someone to push beyond their perceived limitations, realize their full potential and achieve greater success. In a way, you are paying it forward; you can help shape the individual into an effective leader who, in turn, can potentially create a ripple effect of support and growth within their community.

Here are various approaches to help people recognize and nurture their talents:

1. Offer genuine praise, recognizing their strengths, skills, and achievements. Be specific about what you admire in them, so they understand what sets them apart.

2. Offer guidance on areas in which they can improve and help them develop strategies to overcome challenges. Providing constructive feedback without offending someone can be a delicate process. Build a positive relationship and trust with the person before offering feedback and ask if they are open to receiving feedback. Instead of just pointing out the problem, suggest ways they can improve or overcome the issue to demonstrate your intention to help them grow and succeed. Offer praise first, then frame it like this: "You know what would take you to the next level? . . . "

3. Encourage goal setting, which identifies objectives that align with their aspirations. This may entail self-reflection, assessing their values, strengths, weaknesses, and interests. Break down their goals into smaller manageable tasks; prioritize and celebrate milestones with them. Have them develop an action plan, including deadlines, which can help them stay on track, and ask them if they want you to check in on them regularly.

4. Offer resources, such as providing access to tools or opportunities that can help them develop their skills and potential. This could include workshops, mentorship, introducing them to someone, or suggesting books, podcasts, or YouTube videos to consider.

5. Celebrate their achievements, big or small. This will help reinforce their confidence and motivate them to continue pursuing their goals. Celebrating micro wins can release "feel good" chemicals such as dopamine, which contributes to satisfaction and reinforces the actions that led to the success, increasing motivation to pursue further achievements.

Embracing the magnetic quality of recognizing and nurturing the potential in others can transform lives and create a powerful, positive impact on those around you. The most magnetic people are those who selflessly invest in the potential of others, and in turn, they leave an indelible mark on the hearts and minds of everyone they touch. By seeing and nurturing potential in those around you, you not only empower them to achieve their dreams but also create lasting connections that can lead to fruitful partnerships. Unlocking the hidden talents of others will ultimately positively impact those you encounter on your entrepreneurial journey.

Chapter 5 Smart Moves

1. Reflect on the people who have believed in you and the impact they had on your life.

2. Choose two to three people in your life and practice observing and identifying their unique qualities. Offer support and encouragement to them. Also, celebrate their accomplishments.

3. Journal about your relationship and their achievements.

CHAPTER 6

Gratitude Magnet
—Radiating Appreciation and Positivity
How to Build a Life of Gratitude

"Gratitude is a currency that we can mint for ourselves and spend without fear of bankruptcy."

— Fred De Witt Van Amburgh, Publisher and Author

Have you ever had one of those days where you knew you were in a funk, but couldn't seem to shake the feeling? Maybe a meeting didn't go as planned or someone did something that made your heart sink, so now you've decided you're having a terrible day. I was having one of these days, and since I had back-to-back appointments all day, I began wondering if people would be able to sense my "negative vibe." I did some quick research and found that humans can indeed pick up the emotional states of others without verbal communication. I found something referred to as "emotional contagion," the phenomenon of having one person's emotions and behaviors trigger similar emotions in others, where one person's mood can "spread" to others. Therefore, sometimes, a person's general energy level can give off vibes, whether it is positive or negative.

Obviously, I didn't want to give off "negative vibes," so I did what I knew was an antidote for a negative attitude. I started focusing on gratitude, which has always worked for me. Within a matter of minutes, I was able to shake off what I perceived to be a "bad day" and got out of my negative funk. Changing my outlook made me think more about the power of gratitude. Living a life of gratitude can make you magnetic to others. Gratitude is one of the healthiest emotions and our grateful disposition can inspire others to acknowledge or appreciate life's blessings. That's why the practice of gratitude not only enhances our own lives but also positively influences those around us, creating a ripple effect of positivity and magnetism.

Gratitude can play a significant role in building strong business relationships, leading to greater success in the entrepreneurial world. The simple concept of living a life filled with gratitude can guide us toward a life that is potentially brighter, more fulfilling, and enriching, and strengthen our relationships and connections with others. If your business is relationship-based, it makes sense to work towards living a life of gratitude.

Gratitude starts with individual experience and managing your expectations. I think the reason I generally am a grateful person is because I know what it's like to have nothing. I was raised by a single mom; at one point we just had two garbage bags of clothes and a little bit of money my mom had saved for our new life. When we were just getting on our feet, we didn't have a car, so we were thrilled when Safeway opened about a mile from our place. Carrying groceries a mile home was just a way of life, back then. Now that I have experienced having my own vehicle for decades . . . I am embarrassed to admit that I strive for the closest parking spot to the grocery entrance to avoid having to push the grocery cart clear across the parking lot. Why is it that, as humans, we often overlook the fact that many of the things we possess today are the very things we longed for in the past?

This phenomenon is often referred to as "hedonic adaptation" or "the hedonic treadmill" in psychology. This concept suggests that people tend to quickly return to a relatively stable level of happiness despite major positive life events or changes. We adapt to new situations, and over time, what was once new and exciting becomes our new normal.

When we first achieve something we've longed for, maybe a new job, new relationship, or finally buy that dream car or house, we experience an initial burst of excitement. However, over time, as we adapt to this change, the intensity of that excitement may diminish. The achievement becomes part of our everyday reality, and we start taking it for granted.

Furthermore, as human beings, we have a natural tendency to continuously desire more, a phenomenon referred to as the "desire treadmill." Once we obtain something we have yearned for, our focus often shifts to the next thing we want, and we forget to appreciate what we already have.

Cultivating a consistent practice of gratitude can help us counteract these natural tendencies. By consciously acknowledging and appreciating what we have—what we once yearned for—we can maintain a more sustained sense of satisfaction and joy in our lives. Gratitude helps us remember our journey and value the treasures that we have accumulated along the way.

I genuinely believe gratefulness breeds opportunities and has helped me get to where I am today. One of my first "big breaks" came from showing gratitude to someone I least expected would be able to help me launch my business. Early in my career, I had called an insurance carrier, looking for help with a customer service issue. Jeff, the gentleman who helped me, was so kind, helpful, and patient, that after I hung up the phone, I sent him a Starbucks gift card as a small token of my appreciation. What happened after I did that? Jeff started referring hot prospects to me. Unbeknownst to me, he happens to be someone who answers the phone when a prospect calls to apply for coverage, and, at the time, his company didn't have in-house licensed agents. Within about six months, the referrals he sent me accounted for more than $1,000 of reoccurring monthly income! There is no way of fully accounting for how much of my monthly residual income is today a result of his referrals because the clients he sent me ended up referring other clients to me, who also sent their friends to me, and so on. This huge opportunity was the result of my sending a modest gift card, but it was my sincere gratitude and appreciation that I hoped he had felt from me.

You do not have to come from nothing to become a grateful person. Gratitude is like a muscle—the more you exercise it, the stronger it becomes. Here are some ways to cultivate a life of gratitude, even when things don't go your way:

1. **Keep a Gratitude Journal:** Write down three things you're grateful for each day. They don't have to be big things. It could be as simple as beautiful weather, a meaningful conversation from a friend, or a hot shower.

2. **Practice Mindfulness and celebrate small wins:** Mindfulness is about being present in the moment and fully engaging with your current experience. This can help you appreciate small moments of beauty and find small wins to celebrate, even during difficulty.

3. **Reframe Challenges:** Try to see challenges as opportunities for growth. This can be a tough mindset to cultivate, but it can help you see obstacles in a new light.

4. **Express Gratitude to Others:** Let people know when you appreciate them. This not only improves your relationships but can also create a positive feedback loop of gratitude. Write thank you notes, not just when you receive a gift, but also to acknowledge someone's help, kindness, or positive impact in your life. It's rare these days to receive handwritten thank you notes. I have two close people in my life, one of my best friends, Courtney Allen and the wonderful broker on my team, Martina Meinke-Tyler, who not only consistently send handwritten thank you notes, but their children also write thank you notes. It's never expected, but always a nice surprise to get a handwritten thank you card and it makes you stand out!

5. **Focus on What You Can Control:** It's easy to feel overwhelmed and powerless when things go wrong. However, by focusing on what you can control, and being grateful for those areas of autonomy, you can reduce feelings of helplessness.

6. **Seek Positive People:** Surround yourself with people who help you see the good in the world. Their attitudes can be infectious and can help you cultivate your own gratitude.

When your referral partner sends you a client, even if that is your one-hundredth referral for the day, remember back at how excited you were when someone sent you your first referral and respond with that thought in your mind.

Living a life of gratitude does not mean that things always go your way or that life is free from hardships. It means acknowledging and appreciating what is good in your life, regardless of the challenges you might be facing. Gratitude is a shift in perspective. You are not ignoring the hard parts of life, but rather choosing to find light even in the darkness. You could argue that gratitude becomes even more important during difficult times. It can help you shift your focus from what is going wrong to what is going right.

Embracing a life filled with gratitude not only enhances our well-being but also serves as a tool for building meaningful connections and referral partnerships. By cultivating gratitude, we not only recognize the blessings in our lives, but it also can create a ripple effect of positivity that resonates with those around us, which ultimately leads to greater fulfillment in both our personal and professional lives.

Chapter 6 Smart Moves

1.   Start a gratitude journal, listing three things for which you are grateful that day.

2.   Set a daily alarm on your phone to remind you to take a moment during the day to think of something for which you're grateful.

3.   Stock up on some thank you cards from your local store or Amazon and send at least three handwritten out of the blue thank you notes or cards to people you appreciate.

CHAPTER 7

Altruistic Attraction —The Magnetic Power of Serving Others

Discovering the Compelling Force Behind Generosity and Serving Others

"The things you do for yourself are gone when you are gone, but the things you do for others remain as your legacy."

— Kalu Ndukwe Kalu, Political Scientist

Serving others is a huge part of being magnetic. Some of the best leaders are the ones serving their team. We often strive to improve ourselves, to make our lives better, happier, and more fulfilling. We pursue goals and seek recognition, but there's a secret that's often overlooked in our quest for self-improvement—the power of serving others. Service isn't just about doing good for others; it's also a potent tool for personal transformation. This chapter will delve into why serving others makes you magnetic and how you can cultivate this enriching practice.

Let's start with understanding why serving others can make you magnetic. A magnetic individual draws people towards them with their positivity, charisma, and authenticity. People feel comfortable and inspired in their presence. So how does serving others make you magnetic?

1. **Building Authentic Relationships:** Serving others allows us to connect with people on a deeper, more meaningful level. By putting others' needs above our own, we show empathy and kindness, which fosters trust and solidifies bonds.

2. **Developing Personal Growth:** Service provides an opportunity for personal growth. Through serving others, we gain perspectives outside our own, enabling us to become more empathetic, patient, and resilient. This personal growth naturally attracts others as they are drawn to our strength and wisdom.

3. **Exuding Positive Energy:** When we serve others, we experience a sense of fulfillment and happiness, often referred to as the "helper's high." This positivity radiates from us, making us more attractive to others.

4. **Increasing Visibility within the Community:** Engaging in acts of service heightens our visibility in the community. This increased visibility can enhance our reputation, build credibility, demonstrate what you care about, and attract like-minded individuals who value service and community engagement.

Have you heard of the movement "Journey of Generosity (JOG)?" The movement was launched in 2000 by The Maclellan Foundation, with a vision to stir a renewed commitment to generosity amongst Christians through conversations. They host retreats to open conversations surrounding living a life of generosity, without ever asking for a dime from participants, with no strings attached. Friends of mine, David and Robyn Clinton, invited my husband and I to a JOG retreat they hosted and facilitated, where we heard inspirational stories about generous people with giving hearts. I had already considered myself to be a generous person, but the retreat changed my perception on what it means to live a generous life. One company's story stuck out to me . . . Barnhart Crane—their story blew me away. From the beginning, the owners of this company decided to put themselves on a modest salary (they started with a pickup truck, ladder, and welding machine) and committed to turning their profit over to ministries. To give and give like crazy, they donate half their profits to charities. Today they have grown to where they are donating close to $2 million . . . per month! Can you imagine generating the kind of income where after you've paid your expenses and payroll, you are still giving away that kind of money per month? I've heard story after story like this from various entrepreneurs, and they've all had the attitude that "you can't out-give God."

Giving to others does not necessarily mean giving monetarily. You can also give someone your time, by volunteering. Time is a valuable resource you can give that you can never get back. Running an errand, mowing a lawn, or plowing a driveway for a friend who is recovering from surgery, for example.

My mother has always set an example of giving, even when resources were limited. In the late seventies, the Vietnam War had just ended, and due to political repression and social and economic hardships, many Vietnamese people fled the country in search of freedom, including my parents. Due to the risk of being regarded as traitors, the decision to leave the country was often kept secret, as being discovered could result in punishment, including imprisonment. For many, the escape route involved taking a boat to the South China Sea and once on water, the refugees faced numerous dangers, including the threat of pirates, storms, starvation, dehydration, or disease. They knew of the dangers but took the risk of leaving anyway, which was a testament to the profound human desire for freedom and a better life.

In January 1979, my mother and father, in their early twenties, boarded a cargo ship, *Skyluck*, which became known as the ship that smuggled about 2,600 people to freedom. My mom had a friend who took them to the dock, and, at the last minute, they convinced her to flee the country as well. My mom ended up sharing her clothes with her friend, splitting everything down to her undergarments. It ended up being a blessing to my mom because one of the ship crew fell in love with my mom's friend and gave her and my mom a private room to share. This was a big deal because not only did they have a bed to sleep on while everyone else was sleeping on the floor of the cargo ship, but they also had a sink for fresh drinking water. This was another example of how the person giving ends up being blessed.

Through a chain of serendipitous events, there was a remarkable encounter between my family and an American named Gary Murfin, a man unrelated to us by blood but who would come to be known affectionately to us as "Uncle Gary." Living a bachelor's life in his early thirties, Gary received a call—a plea from a Hong Kong Immigration camp seeking assistance for a young couple—my parents—and their newborn daughter, my older sister. Back in those days, agreeing to sponsor immigrants to America meant assuming full financial responsibility to ensure they wouldn't become burdens on society. Despite the weight of this commitment, Gary didn't hesitate. He made the decision to sponsor them, embracing the opportunity to make a meaningful difference in their lives. This act of altruism would ripple through generations. Over the years, he watched proudly as my siblings and I grew and made himself available to walk my sister and I down the aisle at our weddings. Alongside, was Uncle Gary's incredible wife Nancy, who was the epitome of class—compassionate, generous, intelligent, and mentally tough. Her magnetic traits made her an exceptional role model for us.

Our family bonds tightened over the years, with Uncle Gary and Auntie Nancy witnessing our progression into responsible adults and professionals. My sister Helen became a computer engineer, my brother Dean found his passion in medical education, and my sister Laura achieved her doctorate as a physical therapist. Through my Uncle Gary's selfless act, we learned the transformative power of serving others, but he also inspired us to become contributors to society, perpetuating a legacy of compassion and service.

While Uncle Gary's selfless act of sponsoring my family's immigration was extraordinary, it's essential to recognize that such extreme acts of generosity are rare and not the standard expectation for serving others. We need not feel compelled to replicate the magnitude of what Uncle Gary did in order to make a difference in the lives of others.

Serving others doesn't mean losing your identity or always putting others before your own needs. It's about balancing self-care with the desire to help others. Here's how you can cultivate the practice of serving others:

1.   **Start Small:** The thought of serving others may seem overwhelming at first but remember that even the smallest act of kindness can make a difference. Start small, like helping a neighbor or offering a listening ear to a friend in need.

2.   **Identify Your Passions:** Serving others is more meaningful and sustainable when it aligns with your interests and passions. If you love animals, consider volunteering at a local animal shelter. If you're passionate about the environment, join a group that organizes beach cleanups or tree-planting events.

3.   **Join Networking Groups That Focus on Community Service:** Find organizations dedicated to community service. By joining these groups, you can leverage collective efforts to make a larger impact. These organizations often offer a range of opportunities to serve, allowing you to find something that aligns with your interests. Additionally, these groups can be a wonderful way to connect with like-minded individuals who can inspire you and possibly become collaborators in future service projects.

4.   **Encourage Others to Serve:** Inspiring others to serve can expand your impact. Share your experiences and encourage friends, family, and colleagues to join you in serving the community. The ripple effect of this action can be far-reaching.

5.   **Leverage Your Skills:** Everyone possesses unique skills and talents. Identify yours and consider how they might be applied to benefit others. If you're good at teaching, consider tutoring students who are struggling. My husband taught science for over

a decade, so he volunteers to teach hands-on science lessons in Sunday School once a month. If you're a talented cook, you might prepare meals for a local shelter. If you are great at putting together résumés, offer to help job seekers update their résumés.

6. **Serve Virtually:** In our increasingly connected world, there are many opportunities to serve others online. Virtual volunteering can include mentoring, online tutoring, translating documents, or assisting nonprofit organizations with digital tasks.

7. **Random Acts of Kindness:** Cultivate a habit of doing small, spontaneous acts of kindness. This could be as simple as complimenting a stranger, buying coffee for the person behind you in line, or helping a neighbor carry groceries.

By embracing the practice of serving others, we not only enrich our lives but also become a magnetic force that draws people in. It's a win-win situation: we help others, we grow personally, and form authentic connections. Indeed, the power of serving others transforms us into better, more attractive versions of ourselves. We can make a meaningful impact in our communities while forming authentic connections that may lead to fruitful referral partnerships and attract like-minded individuals along the way.

Chapter 7 Smart Moves

1. Consider creating a "random acts of kindness" journal and set goals on how often you would like to perform these acts of kindness.

2. Explore www.GenerousGiving.org and consider getting involved, either virtually or in-person. Participation is entirely cost-free, and they maintain a policy of not soliciting any financial contributions from you. However, it would be beneficial to read about their mission and values beforehand to ensure that their philosophy resonates with your own.

3. Discover or research nonprofit organizations that align with your values through: www.CharityNavigator.org

Magnetic Matchmaker —Magnetizing Connections in a Disconnected World

A Connector's Blueprint to Weaving Lives

"There's a certain magic when two people meet and connect, and you're the reason for that connection."

— Unknown

Have you ever tried setting up two individuals on a date? It has its challenges, but can also be fun, exciting, and intrinsically rewarding. Matchmaking is an art and the ability to match two individuals (with all our human complexities) is a gift. I may have missed my calling as a matchmaker because it brings me so much joy to connect people together. Almost two years ago, I was flying home from a business conference and happened to be on the same flight home as a colleague and friend. And it occurred to me, I should set him up with one of my good friend Katie's sister. I had a feeling they would be a great match. Katie and I started plotting within the next few days to get the two together.

They were both single, the same age, kind, hardworking, and had similar values and faith. Turns out, the two indeed were a perfect match and they hit it off right away. I was ecstatic for them as they went on to get married!

What I did not expect, though, was that their family members would run into me around town and thank me for setting the two up. This made me realize the connection between the two was meaningful, not only to the couple, but also to their families, and they viewed me as a catalyst to making it happen. These two were destined to meet, but I believe God uses people to create connections.

As humans, we are wired for connection, but that is exactly what seems to be lacking these days, with all the noise and distractions we have. I'm not just talking about romantic connections. I am also talking about friendships, as well as business connections. This experience has led me to believe that if you master the art of "people connecting," you can bring joy and happiness into people's lives, and solutions to problems. You are giving people the gift of connection, which is one of our greatest human needs.

If you are known to create connections around town, what ends up happening is that people will regard you in a different light, within your circle of influence and industry. As a "people connector," you create value by introducing people who can help each other professionally. You build trust within your network as a resourceful person, which can elevate your influence on those for whom you have created value. There is also a certain joy you get from helping others. When the connections you facilitate lead to successful friendships, business ventures, job placements, or collaborations, you share in the success indirectly. All it takes is one person to change the trajectory of your life and possibly your family legacy. It has happened over and over again in my life.

My friend Jacklyn Lang, the woman who recruited me into the Medicare field, was someone I interacted with for about a month at my previous job in the mortgage industry. We stayed connected through social media, but years later, she called me out of the blue to talk about the insurance industry, which changed my world forever.

What if you introduced someone to a friend that resulted in a change in their trajectory and life?

In this chapter, we will discuss the practice of becoming a "people connector" so that you can become known as someone who opens doors, creates opportunities, and helps others succeed, which can be a powerful part of your personal brand.

The art of connecting others involves developing several skills and traits, while adhering to certain principles. Here are some skills you can practice to become a people connector:

1. **Observation Skills:** Developing observation skills means cultivating the ability to notice, understand, and interpret those around you. It means being attuned to human behavior, recognizing patterns, and making connections based on what you observe; having a keen intuition and a deep understanding of people's needs and desires to see potential connections that others may overlook. One of the best ways you can practice and develop observation skills is spending time "people watching." Obviously, you're not doing so in a creepy way, but think of it as a master class in human behavior, a way to gather insights about human behavior, dynamics, and interpersonal relationships. Observing people can refine your ability to notice subtle details by enhancing your observational abilities. Start by choosing locations with a good mix of activities, such as parks, malls, restaurants, or other public gathering spots. Be discreet and observe without making anyone feel uncomfortable or drawing attention to yourself. You can have

a book, journal, or cup of coffee in hand to blend in. Take in the entire scene before focusing on specific individuals or groups. Pay attention to body language, facial expressions, gestures, and posture. Instead of making immediate judgments, take a moment to reflect on why someone might behave in a certain way. Try to deduce relationships between people. Are they friends, family, or strangers and what might be the nature and depth of their relationship? As an exercise, you can try to weave a short narrative or backstory based on your observations. After observing a situation or person, share your observations with a trusted friend or mentor and get feedback on your insights. People watching can help you refine and improve your observation skills over time. Understanding personal dynamics, including how certain personalities mesh or clash, can help you introduce individuals with complementary personalities or shared interests.

2. **Problem Solving:** Problem solving is an invaluable skill which enables you to identify potential complementary traits, opportunities, and common ground in connections, as well as gaps and mismatches. An adept problem solver will read between the lines, making connections based on talents, unvoiced desires, or future potential. Steps to practicing problem solving, relevant to people connecting, include using active listening skills to identify a friend's or family's need, gathering relevant information related to that need, brainstorming various solutions (including who they could connect with that could help them), evaluating and implementing the solution, or facilitating the introduction. Imagine your brain as an expansive filing cabinet, each drawer containing folders labeled with names, skills, experiences, and solutions. Every time you meet someone new or acquire new information, you're adding a new file or updating an existing one. When someone presents you with a need, it's like being handed a query slip for your filing cabinet. You need to find the right file that could

potentially contain the solution. With the problem in hand, you rummage through the files in your mental filing cabinet. This means recollecting individuals you know who have the expertise, resources, or desire that matches that current need. Every new person you meet or every new skill you learn about someone adds to your filing system, enhancing your problem-solving capability. The broader and more diverse your filing cabinet, the more equipped you are to address an array of challenges.

3. **Building a Large Network:** Building a network and being a "people connector" are intrinsically linked concepts, while amplifying the value of the other. Building a network is about establishing connections and relationships, which involves knowing people and understanding their passions and interests. Being a people connector is about taking your networking a step further, actively introducing individuals within your network to each other, based on mutual interests, needs, or potential synergies. Having a large and diverse network will maximize opportunities to help connect people to others.

Ways to build your network include:

A. Attending networking events and conferences, while connecting with new people at these events.

B. Engaging online and social media platforms, including joining relevant groups on Facebook or other social networks. Not engaging with others on social media is like going to a party and not talking to anyone there.

C. Diversifying your network by going beyond your immediate industry or field, which can open unexpected doors and offer unique perspectives.

D. Providing value to others by sharing knowledge, providing assistance, or offering resources. When you are seen as a valuable connection, people will want to connect with you.

E.   Host social events or get-togethers. My husband Chris hosts a monthly guys' night as a way for men to fellowship and encourage each other. Many friendships have formed within this group of men who have connected with each other.

F.   Engaging in public speaking and workshops. Presenting at events or conducting workshops can quickly amplify your visibility and credibility, prompting more people to connect with you.

G.   Collaborating on projects with others, whether they are work projects or community efforts, can expand your network.

H.   Volunteering by offering your skills or time to causes can introduce you to people from varied backgrounds and industries.

I.   Engaging in local community activities such as town hall meetings, local clubs, or participating in community-driven activities. In my town, Adam Schluter started a movement called "Monday Night Dinners," where he invites strangers to gather in his backyard every Monday night to enjoy a potluck-style community dinner. He makes it very clear that it's not a business networking group, with no motives other than to connect with others in the community. He hires a local band to play live music that evening and suggests a $10 donation from each guest to support the local artist. Currently, more than one thousand people have joined his Facebook group and I believe over a hundred people gather at his place for each Monday Night Dinner. I can't even imagine how many friendships and connections have stemmed from this tradition of his. I am Facebook friends with Adam and have observed any time he has asked for a recommendation or needed minor help with something, he always has a ton of people jumping in to help or introduce him to someone who can help. His willingness to try something new and creative has made him a "people connector," which not only created a network for himself, but also for those who attend his community dinners.

Be genuine and authentic. If people feel you are genuinely interested in their well-being and success, they are likely to respect and appreciate you; an authentic people connector does not hide behind ulterior motives. They connect people because they genuinely believe it will be of mutual benefit. If you're genuine in your understanding and intentions, the less likely it is that you'll connect with the wrong people. You're not just connecting for the sake of expanding your network; you're connecting to create value. In a world overflowing with transient interactions and fleeting connections, authenticity and genuineness stand out. As a "people connector," these traits ensure that your introductions are rooted in sincerity and the genuine desire to add value to others' lives. When you position yourself with authenticity, you not only enhance your magnetic pull but also elevate the quality and impact of the connections you facilitate.

As far as "people connecting" etiquette, there are certain Dos and Don'ts:

Dos: Obtain permission before introducing two individuals, to show respect for their time and interest. Provide each party with some information about the other and why you believe the connection could be beneficial. If someone shares confidential or personal information with you, do not pass this on without permission.

Don'ts: Don't force connections. You might see potential for a connection, but if either party isn't interested or ready, don't push it. Don't connect only to gain; your primary motive should be to assist others. Don't ignore feedback; if someone tells you a connection wasn't helpful or was negative, use it as an opportunity to improve your matching process. Remember, connecting others is an art form; it's about recognizing synergies, reading unspoken needs, and predicting the potential alchemy of relationships. At its core, this endeavor calls for authenticity, keen observation, and a genuine heart that finds joy in others' happiness and success. Such actions not only can create ripples in the lives of those directly connected but also etch a mark of trust and gratitude upon the connector's life story. By honing observational skills, expanding your network, sharpening problem-solving abilities, and embodying authenticity, you position yourself as a beacon in a disconnected world, by merging lives and destinies. Each connection is unique and as you learn more about people and their needs and their interests, you will continue to grow as a connector. By embracing this role with heart and purpose, you are not just fostering relationships; you're reigniting the essence of human connectivity in an increasingly fragmented world. Becoming a skilled people connector not only enriches the lives of those you bring together but also enhances your own reputation and influence within your community and industry. You create meaningful connections that lead to friendships, collaborations, and opportunities. Remember, connecting others is an art form rooted in genuine care and understanding, and by embracing this role, you become a catalyst for positive change in a world longing for human connection.

Chapter 8 Smart Moves

1. Spend thirty minutes at a local park, mall, or other public location to "people watch" and observe.

2. Choose three action items from the list under #3 "Building a large network" to help build your network and visibility.

CHAPTER 9

Digital Allure —Captivating Prescence in the Digital Realm

Strategies for Elevating Your Social Media Presence

"Content is fire; social media is gasoline."

–Jay Baer, Author and Speaker

My business would not be where it is today if it were not for social media. Thanks to online platforms, I was able to connect with and organically build a network of referral partners who have sent me business, which allowed me to expand nationwide. Social media presence was one of the things I struggled with because I initially didn't believe in attention-seeking posts. I was always taught self-attention-seeking was a bad thing. Furthermore, if you are a business owner trying to catch the attention of potential prospects, standing out on social media is like trying to be heard in a crowded stadium, which can be overwhelming with everyone shouting at once.

Then I heard this saying that was an "aha moment" for me . . . Coach Micheal Burt declared at a conference I attended, "It's not the best product that wins, it's the best *marketed* product that wins." If what you provide is a service, you *are* the product . . . you are the brand. That was when I realized the importance of effectively leveraging social media presence to drive significant business growth.

If you are an individual proprietor, having a strong social media presence based only on your personal page can offer a multitude of benefits, even if you rarely post about your services and products. This is because you invite people to get to know you, to cultivate the "know, like, and trust" factor, which is instrumental in converting followers into loyal customers.

Non-social media engagement (or being a "lurker") is like going to a networking event or party and standing in the corner by yourself. Mastering social media presence is an art and takes time to build. Here are my top observations and strategies for positioning yourself on social media:

1. The benefits of leveraging your personal Facebook page for business purposes:

> A) **Direct Engagement:** Interacting with your audience on a personal level can lead to more authentic and meaningful connections. It allows for direct conversations, fostering a sense of community and loyalty.
> B) **Building Trust:** Sharing behind-the-scenes content, successes, challenges, and stories related to your business can humanize your brand and build trust among your audience.

C) **Broader Reach:** Friends and family on your personal account are more likely to engage with and share your posts, increasing your organic reach and potentially introducing your business to a wider audience.

D) **Increased Visibility:** Business pages often suffer from reduced organic reach due to Facebook algorithms. Posts from your personal pages are more likely to appear in your friends' news feeds, ensuring higher visibility for your content.

E) **Feedback:** Sharing new product ideas or seeking feedback is easier. Friends and family might provide honest feedback that could be invaluable for your business.

2. The Facebook algorithm is pretty straightforward. It aims to show you content that you genuinely care about. The more you engage with someone's posts by liking, commenting, or sharing, the more Facebook thinks it's relevant to you. Your close friends and family's content usually shows up first, and posts with a lot of interactions also get priority. Newer posts and videos tend to get a boost too. Essentially, the more interactive and recent the content, the higher its chances of popping up on your feed. Therefore, if you want to stay visible on your friends' walls, you have to post things that grab their attention. Engaging content isn't just for fun—it's a strategy. The more your posts resonate with people, the more likely they are to pop up on their feeds. So, the key is to keep it engaging and keep it relevant.

3. Certain types of content are more engaging and likely to make people pay attention. In general, people pay attention when you make them think, laugh, solve problems, surprise them, make

them feel understood, or inspire them. The types of content that are most engaging are:

A) **Videos:** Tutorials and how-tos, behind-the-scenes, testimonials, reviews, and interviews.

B) **Humor and Memes:** Ensure they align with your brand.

C) **Interactive Contents:** Quizzes, polls, and interactive infographics.

D) **Timely and Relevant Content:** Creating content around trending topics and news, or seasonal content or campaigns.

E) **Listicles and Curated Content:** "Top 10" lists and curated resources or tools.

F) **User-Generated Content:** Testimonials, user reviews, photos shared by users.

G) **Challenges and Contests:** Dance, song, or caption challenges.

H) **Emotional or Story-Driven Content:** Inspirational or motivational posts, personal or brand-origin stories.

4. Record videos. Recording video significantly enhances one's digital presence, as exemplified by my industry friend Christian Brindle. Four years ago, Christian started his YouTube journey, committing to consistent video uploads, even when he didn't feel like recording videos. Presently, with nearly one thousand videos and over five thousand subscribers, his channel stands as a testament to the power of video content. Interestingly, Christian often interviews competitors on his channel, fostering collaboration and community within his industry. In an episode where I'm a guest on his show, we discuss creating videos. He emphasizes that through video, audiences develop a sense of familiarity and connection, which can build loyalty. His advice to aspiring video

creators is simple: don't overthink it. Just speak to the camera as if you're engaging in a casual conversation. It's just you and this little dot that you're staring into for the camera. It's about establishing a genuine connection with your audience.

My friend Erik Allen has recorded hundreds of podcasts and his show, "The Erik Allen Show" is now ranked in the top 1.5% of all podcasts globally! He wrote a book and built a self paced course on how to start a podcast, which includes everything you need to know about launching a podcast. You can find his resources here: ErikAllenMedia.com/resources-podcasting

5. Master the art of storytelling. Michael McCormick from Insurance Soup™ has been teaching his clients the value of storytelling. A well-told story can evoke emotions, and people tend to remember how something made them feel more than the details of what was said. Sharing genuine stories, especially those that show vulnerability or behind-the-scenes insights, can foster trust and credibility with your audience. If you consistently share insightful, valuable stories related to your niche, it can position you as an authority or thought leader in your field.

Michael came up with a simple formula for master storytelling: Fact + Emotion + Action.

> A) **A Story Is a FACT:** At the heart of every compelling story is a core fact or a central truth. This fact serves as the foundation upon which the entire narrative is built. Without a concrete fact or a genuine event, the story lacks substance and authenticity. For example, you might share a story about how your product helped a customer achieve something significant.

B) **Wrapped in EMOTION:** How do you wrap a fact in emotion? You make it relatable to a human need or desire. Facts on their own can be dry and may not resonate with your audience. But when these facts are wrapped in emotion (through relatable experiences or powerful imagery), they become memorable. Emotions create a connection between the storyteller and the audience, making the story relatable and impactful. For example, using the story above, instead of just stating the fact, you may add an emotional layer by detailing your client's struggles before using your product and/or her feelings of frustration and the relief and happiness she felt after seeing the results.

C) **That Compels Us to Take ACTION:** A masterful story doesn't just end with the reader feeling something; it moves them to do something! This action might be to buy a product, change a perspective, support a cause, or any number of other actions. The story's call-to-action is a testament to its effectiveness. For example, after hearing your client's transformation with your product, the audience might feel compelled to try the product for themselves or share your story with someone who might benefit from it.

The first time I followed Michael's formula to a tee . . . I shared how my parents escaped from a communist country, added emotional elements, and the call to action was encouraging people who have faced adversity and discrimination (because we've all faced some sort of discrimination in our lifetime) to use it to fuel a fire to succeed in life. Within a day or so, over a 120 people shared that post. I have had several people, including clients, reach out and invite me to dinner to hear more about that story.

6. Engaging with your audience is a cornerstone of building a loyal and interactive community on social media. Here are ways to engage with them:

A. **Direct Interactions:** Respond to comments, messages, and mentions. Host Q and A or "Ask Me Anything" sessions.

B. **Collaborations and Takeovers:** Allow an influencer or prominent figure in your niche to take over your media account for a day. Collaborate with other brands or influencers on joint content or events.

C. **Go Live:** Use live streaming to interact with your audience in real time.

D. **Host Events:** Organize webinars, workshops, or meetups (virtually or physically) and invite your audience.

E. **Feedback Solicitation:** Ask for feedback on your products, services, or content.

7. Strike a balance when merging personal and professional content. Overemphasizing business can dilute the authenticity of your personal page and alienate your audience. Blending boundaries between personal and professional content can risk unintentional oversharing, revealing too much personal information to a wider audience. Friends and family who primarily engage with your personal updates might find frequent business posts disengaging or perceive them as spam. To manage this, you might consider using platform tools, like Facebook's "custom audiences," to segment posts, ensuring business-related content reaches the appropriate audience without overshadowing personal interactions. The key is to maintain authenticity while being both strategic and considerate.

It's evident that a compelling presence online is both an art and a science. Jay Baer's metaphor encapsulates this perfectly: "Content is fire; social media is gasoline." Content is fire; high-quality content can engage, enlighten, and draw people in. Content serves as the foundational element, the core message, or the main attraction. Social media is gasoline; gasoline, when added to fire, makes it burn brighter and spread faster. Similarly, social media platforms amplify content, allowing it to reach a wider audience at a much faster rate. It takes what's already burning (your content) and magnifies its impact, making it more visible and influential. Without fire, gasoline is just a liquid; without content, social media lacks substance. Conversely, a fire without gasoline might not spread as fast or burn as bright; content without social media might not reach its full audience potential. In the end, your digital presence should reflect a genuine composite of who you are and the value you bring. Embrace your digital allure, but with a touch of authenticity, strategy, and mindfulness.

Mastering social media presence is essential for modern business growth, allowing you to connect authentically with your audience, build trust, and expand your network of potential referral partners. Remember, social media is both an art and a science, requiring authenticity, strategy, and mindfulness to make a lasting impact in today's digital landscape.

Chapter 9 Smart Moves

1. Practice the art of storytelling. Share a personal story on social media, using Michael McCormick's formula: Fact + Emotion + Action. Journal the stories you share and the engagement you observe.

2. For a week, before posting, categorize each piece of content, tracking the types of content you post and the engagement (likes, shares, comments). Pay attention to which content categories are performing best and, based on your findings, adjust. You may ask your audience for feedback. What type of content would they like to see more of?

CHAPTER 10

Igniting Your Charisma For Magnetic Connections
The Charismatic Path to Genuine Connections

"Charisma is not so much getting people to like you as getting people to like themselves when you're around."

–Robert Breault, Musician

In the world of business, where connections can make or break your success, being seen as a go-to referral partner isn't just about flaunting your achievements. It's more about making genuine connections and standing out in a packed room. The secret sauce ingredient to standing out is charisma. Charisma is that unique sparkle that builds trust, creates influence, and cultivates connections. Think of charisma as your silent partner—it opens doors before you even knock on them and can cement relationships before any contract is signed. The good news is, even if you were not born with charisma, it's something that can be developed over time!

Think of someone you know who has charisma. Can you pinpoint what it is about the person that screams charismatic? Vanessa Van

Edwards, one of my favorite writers, authored an interesting book called *Cues* that define charisma. Charisma is the perfect combination of competence and warmth. Lack of charisma is usually due to some sort of imbalance between those two things. If you are competent but lack warmth, people view you as intimidating. If you are a super warm person but lack competence, people will not take you seriously. If people often tell you that you can be intimidating, work on being more "warm." If people often dismiss you and don't take you seriously, work on appearing more competent.

You can take inventory to gauge if people view you as competent, warm, or both by Googling characteristics that describe a warm and then a competent person. Take note and tally all the words you see that you have heard people use to describe you. For example, words that describe a warm person might be "trustworthy, friendly, kind, compassionate, thoughtful, a team player." Words that describe competence might be "impressive, powerful, smart, an expert, a leader."

Based on your characteristics inventory, you can determine if you should work on presenting yourself as more competent, warm, or both.

Here are some examples of how to improve your warmth and competence:

Creating Warmth:

1. **Active Listening:** Truly listen to people when they speak without interrupting or formulating a response while they're still talking. Oprah Winfrey is renowned for her empathetic interviewing style. When guests speak, she fully engages with them, making them feel heard and understood, a key reason why many share deep personal stories on her shows.

2.   **Provide Genuine Compliments:** Offer sincere praise without expecting anything in return. Dwayne "The Rock" Johnson is widely recognized for his uplifting and positive nature. On social media and in interviews, he consistently compliments and praises his costars, team members, and fans. His sincere appreciation for others contributes to his massive global appeal and the affectionate rapport he maintains with his fans.

3.   **Showing Empathy:** Put yourself in others' shoes and respond with understanding and compassion. Princess Diana was often called "The People's Princess" because of her genuine compassion and understanding for people from all walks of life. Showing empathy helps people feel emotionally safe around you.

4.   **Maintain Open Body Language:** Make eye contact, smile, use approachable demeanor, and lean in slightly when conversing. George Clooney has been noted for his charismatic presence in public appearances and interviews. His relaxed posture, engaging eye contact, and genuine smiles make those with whom he interacts feel instantly at ease and connected, which has cemented his reputation as one of Hollywood's most personable and approachable celebrities.

5.   **Relatability:** Share personal stories and find common ground with others. Keanu Reeves is often described as one of the most down-to-earth celebrities. Despite his wealth, he is known to live relatively modestly and has been spotted multiple times using public transportation. There's a well-circulated story of Keanu spending an evening with a group of homeless people, sitting down with them, sharing food, and just talking for hours. Keanu has faced significant personal tragedies, including the loss of a child and the untimely death

of a longtime partner. He's spoken openly about grief and how these losses have shaped him, allowing many who've experienced similar losses to feel connected to him. Being relatable bridges gaps and helps establish a mutual bond with others.

Creating Competence:

1. **Demonstrate Expertise and Skill Mastery:** Share your knowledge and skills without being boastful, by sharing stories instead of achievements. Share about your journey, challenges, and learning experiences. This shifts the focus from "look what I did" to "here's what I learned." J.K. Rowling, the renowned author of the *Harry Potter* series, is one of the bestselling authors in history. Yet, instead of merely highlighting the phenomenal success of her books, she has often shared her personal story of facing rejections, battling depression, and being a single mother on welfare before her big break. People tend to trust individuals who exhibit humility with their expertise.

2. **Communicate Effectively:** Articulate your thoughts clearly and concisely, speak with confidence but avoid arrogance. Elon Musk, despite his ventures into diverse fields from electric cars to space exploration, can break down complex ideas into understandable terms for the public. Communicating effectively ensures people understand and value your contributions.

3. **Confidence:** Believe in your abilities and tackle tasks with assurance, without arrogance. Initially famous as a WWE wrestler, Dwayne "The Rock" Johnson faced criticism and significant challenges of changing professional lanes from sports entertainment to cinema, but persevered with the belief that he could become a

leading actor. His approach to tackling new roles and taking on new challenges with confidence without arrogance, makes him a great example of how confidence can be contagious; others will believe in you if you believe in yourself.

4. **Reliability:** Always follow through on commitments and promises. Warren Buffett, the Chairman and CEO of Berkshire Hathaway, is known not only for his investing expertise but also for his reliability and trust worthiness. Since taking over Berkshire Hathaway, Buffet has been writing annual letters to shareholders which provide insights into the company's performance, investment philosophy, and often life lessons. The letter has been an annual tradition for more than six decades and has become a must read for investors around the globe. He has always emphasized the importance of ethics in business. He famously said, "It takes twenty years to build a reputation and five minutes to ruin it." Being reliable solidifies your reputation as a trust-worthy individual.

5. **Be Well-Prepared:** Show up to meetings prepared, which will enhance your credibility, increase efficiency, and instill confidence in your audience or collaborators. Steve Jobs, cofounder of Apple, was known for his meticulous preparation for product launches. Before the famous iPhone unveiling in 2007, he rehearsed exhaustively. He anticipated potential glitches and worked with his team to ensure every moment of the presentation was choreographed to perfection. Every slide, word, and product demo were precisely timed. This level of preparedness resulted in some of the tech industry's most iconic product launches and solidified his reputation as a master presenter.

In the previous chapters, I have handpicked topics that will help you naturally build other warmth and competence cues and how to strike a balance between the two. As your charisma grows, and you find the perfect balance between the two, so will your magnetic appeal. In today's business landscape, where true connections are invaluable currency, charisma becomes a magnetic force to create lasting impressions and build bridges. While credentials have their place, they can't compare to the allure of genuine charisma. By blending warmth with competence, not only will you distinguish yourself, but you position yourself as the ideal referral partner everyone seeks. In today's competitive landscape, charisma sets you apart and positions you as the ideal collaborator everyone wants to work with.

Chapter 10 Smart Moves

1. Google "traits of a warm person" and "traits of a competent person" and take inventory by listing the characteristics that people often use to describe you. This will help you determine if you need to work on warmth or competence traits to balance.

2. Focus on at least one of the skills or characteristics you would like to improve and journal when you have been intentional with building that trait. Journal your progress and self-reflection.

CHAPTER 11

Courage Over Caution —Rising Above the Fear of Rejection

Navigating Rejection in the Quest for Referral Partners

"Most fears of rejection rest on the desire for approval from other people. Don't base your self-esteem on their opinions."

–Harvey Mackay, American Businessman

A t the core of much of our hesitation, inaction, and reluctance in the business world is the fear of rejection. While this fear is common, especially when reaching out to potential referral partners, it's important to remember that it often is a self-imposed barrier to our own success. So why do we harbor this fear in the first place? Personal experiences, particularly past rejections or embarrassments, may heighten our sensitivity. Also, we often tend to amplify the potential outcomes of rejection, imagining worst-case scenarios. These imagined outcomes are rarely, if ever, as severe as we envision. Embracing rejection, rather than dreading it, is pivotal to positive reinforcement to our success. Seeing rejection as a stepping stone, rather than a setback, propels our journey to success. Numerous individuals have faced rejection in their journeys to success. Their stories serve as inspirational reminders that rejection is often just a steppingstone to achieving greatness:

- ✧ Colonel Harland Sanders, the founder of KFC, faced rejection more than 1,000 times while trying to franchise his fried chicken recipe. He traveled across the U.S., receiving numerous "no" responses, before finally finding a partner. Today, KFC is a global fast food chain, one of the most successful companies in the world.

- ✧ Before building the Disney empire, Walt Disney faced numerous rejections. He was once fired from a newspaper for "lacking imagination" and "having no original ideas." His first animation company went bankrupt. Instead of succumbing to these setbacks, Disney persisted, leading to the creation of the global brand we know today.

- ✧ Stephen King's debut novel, *Carrie*, was rejected thirty times before it was published. He had thrown away the manuscript in frustration, but his wife retrieved it and encouraged him to keep trying. Not only was *Carrie* published but it also became a massive hit, cementing King's position as a master of horror fiction.

- ✧ Before Oprah Winfrey became a media mogul, she faced rejection and was even fired from her job as a television reporter because she was deemed "unfit for TV." Instead of giving in to this assessment, she channeled her passion into creating a talk show empire.

Each of these people faced rejection numerous times; yet they did not let fear of further rejection deter them. Their stories prove that persistence, passion, and self-belief can overcome even the harshest rejections. Here are some strategies you can use to overcome the fear of rejection:

1. Shift Your Mindset: We often interpret rejection as a personal flaw or inadequacy, when sometimes, it becomes evident that there are other factors at play, many of which are external and beyond our control. Have you heard about the restaurant analogy? Imagine you're deciding where to eat dinner tonight. You have a whole list of options—Italian, Japanese, Mexican, American, and so on. After some thought, you decide on Italian. Does this mean you have rejected all other cuisines? Not at all. You've chosen what best suits your needs or cravings at this particular moment. In the same way, when someone decides not to partner with you or turns down your proposal, it doesn't mean they're rejecting you as a person or even the value you bring. They are simply choosing what they believe is the best fit for their current situation, needs, or goals. The key takeaways from this analogy are:

> A) **Mismatched Needs, Not Rejection:** Just as you can't eat at every restaurant at the same time, people can't say yes to every proposal or opportunity that comes their way. Their "no" may be more about their own constraints or current needs rather than a judgment about your worth or capabilities.
>
> B) **Timing Matters:** Sometimes you're in the mood for tacos, sometimes for pizza. In business, sometimes the timing is just off. Maybe your potential referral partner is overwhelmed with current commitments. That doesn't mean a collaboration is off the table forever. Circumstances and appetites change.
>
> C) **Opportunity for Future Engagement:** Even if you don't pick a certain restaurant tonight, it doesn't

mean you'll never eat there. Similarly, a "no" today doesn't mean a "no" forever in a business context. Keep the door open for future opportunities.

D) Not a reflection of your worth: Shifting your mindset lies in understanding that rejection isn't a reflection of your worth but rather a matter of current circumstances, needs, and perspectives. So, the next time you experience the fear of rejection, remember the restaurant analogy.

2. Mel Robbin's "Five Second Rule:" A transformational technique she developed to prompt action, overcoming procrastination and hesitation, and to change behaviors. The concept is simple, yet powerful. Whenever you have an impulse to act on a goal or task, count backwards from five to one and then immediately act before your brain can talk you out of it.

Robbin's inspiration for the rule came during a challenging time in her life when she was struggling with depression and found it difficult to get out of bed and was dreading the day ahead. One evening, she saw a commercial featuring a rocket launching, which gave her an idea. She decided the next morning that she would "launch" herself out of bed like a rocket by counting down from five and then moving, which interrupted her habitual pattern of hitting the snooze button, which then provided momentum. She began to use the Five Second Rule in other areas of her life, from making business calls she had been avoiding to pushing herself to network. She found this technique to be effective, so she began sharing this strategy through speeches and a book she wrote titled *The 5 Second Rule*, which resonated with many people worldwide. The act of counting backward can interrupt negative thought cycles and shift the focus. By the time you reach "one," you are primed to act, instead of dwelling on the task, which gives your brain time to conjure doubts and fears. For example, you're at a networking event and spot a potential referral partner. Instead of hesitating, debating internally whether to approach them and potentially talking yourself out of doubt, you'd count "five, four, three, two, one," and start walking towards that person. This rapid action leaves no room for self-doubt.

3. Grit and the Power of One More: grit is the tenacious spirit that drives individuals to persevere through challenges, setbacks, and the temptation to give up in the most trying times and is intrinsically tied to conquering the fear of rejection. It's the unwavering commitment to a long-term goal, combined with the resilience to push through adversity. Ed Mylett's "power of one more" encapsulates this essence of grit beautifully. Drawing inspiration from his father, a recovering alcoholic who committed to sobriety "one more day" at a time, Mylett applied the same principle to his professional struggles. Before he rose to prominence as a motivational speaker, Mylett faced moments of doubt and considered quitting. However, reminded by his father's words, he chose not to quit for "just one more day," propelling him ahead and turning challenges into stepping stones towards his ultimate success.

4. Positive Affirmations: Affirmations are positive reinforcements that can rewire our thought patterns. By focusing on past successes and our inherent strengths, we can validate our self-belief and diminish the fear of rejection. For example, before a crucial meeting, remind yourself of past accomplishments: "I spearheaded the XYZ project that led to a 30 percent increase in sales," or, "I've successfully collaborated with several partners in the past and this is another opportunity to do so."

5. Embracing Divine Protection: Jamie Kern Lima, the cofounder of IT Cosmetics, often uses the phrase, "Rejection is God's Protection." It reframes rejection as a form of guidance, suggesting that when a door closes, it may be divinely intended to steer you in a direction that's for your betterment. Perhaps the opportunity wasn't right, or there's something better waiting around the corner. Jamie is now on the *Forbes'* Richest Self-Made Women list, but her road to success was far from smooth. She literally heard hundreds of "noes" from every beauty retailer and faced rejection for more than three years, but she never gave up and figured out how not to take rejection personally. Incorporating the philosophy of "Rejection is God's Protection" encourages resilience and trust in the face of setbacks and assures that every rejection is a redirection towards a path more aligned with your purpose or destiny.

I realize I have just written an entire chapter surrounding the topic of rejection . . . but notice these are all strategies on how to overcome *the fear* of rejection. The chapter title is not "Overcoming Rejection," because the reality is, when it comes to seeking referral partners, it's highly unlikely you will face rejection from potential referral partners. Keep in mind, most professionals are in the same boat: seeking to expand their networks, grow their business, and cultivate meaningful relationships. For example, you're a real estate agent who wants to partner with a local interior designer to provide a more holistic service to your clients. Remember, it's not just you who stands to gain; the interior designer also gets access to a new customer base without having to market aggressively. Partnerships can be a win-win, potentially offering both professionals increased revenue and market share. Recognizing the mutual benefits can dispel the notion that you're asking for a favor. Instead, you're proposing a collaboration that could add value to both sides.

Also, keep in mind that if you reach out to a potential referral partner, but they decline, maybe because of their existing commitment to a similar partnership, it doesn't mean the end of the road for you. For every potential partner who is not interested in partnering with you, numerous others may be looking for someone with your skill set and offerings. Remember that the professional landscape is fertile ground for collaborations. Most likely, your colleagues and competitors are looking for the same thing you are—meaningful connections that can help everyone involved reach new heights of success.

Chapter 11 Smart Moves

1. Practice Mel Robbins' 5 Second Rule once a day. Incorporate it into a personal or business task that you usually dread or procrastinate doing. The moment you feel the urge to contact a potential referral partner, count down five seconds and execute the task. Practice affirmation: Before approaching your potential referral partner, visualize a positive interaction to boost your confidence. Mindset matters, so going into a situation with a positive outlook can often influence the outcome more than you might expect.

CHAPTER 12

The Accountability Effect
—A Paradigm for Excellence
Driving Excellence Through Accountability

"Accountability is the glue that ties commitment to the result."

— Bob Proctor, Author

Every endeavor worth pursuing usually includes detours, setbacks, and sometimes, the temptation to quit. Willpower is abundant at the beginning of your journey, but when the initial excitement wears off, your willpower to push through starts to decline. Sometimes a little success could even cause you to take your foot off the pedal when you still have a way to get to the finish line. So, what then separates a successful journey from a futile one? The answer, quite simply, is accountability.

Without accountability, even the most committed individuals can find themselves adrift, their goals unfulfilled, and their potential untapped. On the flip side, accountability ensures that your commitment is more than just a wish or aspiration. It transforms it into actionable steps that lead to measurable outcomes.

I was eating dinner with my friend Katie, and she asked me, "How is your book coming along?" I had only told a handful of people at that point, but I had previously told Katie that I was quietly working on writing a book. However, it took me a lot longer than expected to get through my first draft. Life gets demanding; I am a busy mom with an insurance agency to run. Staying on top of industry changes and regulations is a job in itself! Unfortunately, the excuses are endless. After Katie asked me about my book, I proudly reported that I was on my last chapter. However, I did not tell her it had been about a month since I finished writing the previous chapter. She's very encouraging when she hears about my progress, and I could see she was excited for me. So, guess what happened? I got back to writing, working on my final chapter. This brief exchange with Katie was enough to push me towards the finish line. This is a minor example of the benefits of having an accountability partner or someone who holds you responsible for meeting commitments and deadlines. Setting up accountability sometimes feels uncomfortable, but it sets you up for success with whatever you are trying to accomplish.

This chapter will explore the role of accountability, a tool for achieving success. We will discuss ways to build and maintain accountability, such as tracking progress, creating milestones, seeking mentorship, and leveraging public accountability through platforms like Google reviews. We will also discuss how accountability can serve as the foundation for building strong referral partners, creating a network of individuals who are as committed to your success as you are to theirs.

Reflecting on the jobs that I previously held, when I worked in the mortgage industry for my brother-in-law Vince McPhail, we had the most robust system of accountability processes in place. At any given moment, he could "y jack" into my calls to listen in on my conversations. We had weekly team meetings where everyone would list deals they were working on the whiteboard. We had monthly one-on-one meetings with Vince to set goals, review our performance, and discuss ways we could have improved if we fell short of our goals. It was not a coincidence that my colleagues and I became award-winning account executives and were consistently the top performing branch in the district, and we were often recognized at the state level as well. It was the most accountability I have ever had out of all my jobs. In fact, it was on this job that I won many trips, recognitions, and plaques. When I think of all the types of accountabilities there are, I see most of these were implemented when I worked under Vince.

Here are the several types of accountabilities to explore and figure out which type works best for you:

1. Self-Accountability

Self-accountability involves setting your own goals, tracking your progress, and rewarding yourself, based on your performance. My brother-in-law Vince believed having rewards and consequences are foundational to the principle of accountability. When individuals know they will face consequences for their actions or inactions, they are more likely to take ownership of their decisions. A reward could be as simple as treating yourself to a fancy drink from your favorite coffee shop, buying that item you've had your eye on, or pampering yourself with a massage, facial, or pedicure when you have hit certain goals. Tools like goal-setting apps, journals, or spreadsheets can be helpful. Self-accountability does not require external resources, therefore it is cost-effective, while giving you the flexibility to set your own rules and pace. The downside would be the lack of external pressure makes it easier to slack off and sometimes you are not the best judge of your own performance. It's rare to have consequences in place as a self-employed person, with no "boss." However, maybe the consequence is that you don't reach your goals as quickly as you would like. This is why it is important to figure out, know, and write down your "whys." One of my mentors and friends, Andrew Strange, a successful serial entrepreneur, gave me an assignment during our first few conversations: to figure out my "whys." He emphasized this task as one of the most crucial steps that helped him navigate his entrepreneurial journey. At the core of your meaningful endeavor lies the "why"—the reason(s) or motivation driving an action. It's the desire and burning passion or purposeful intent that pushes you forward. Knowing your "why" keeps your motivation and willpower alive, even through challenging times.

2. Peer Accountability

Pair up with a friend or colleague who has similar goals or is someone who's achievements or work ethic you admire. Networking events is a great way to find like-minded individuals, especially events related to your industry. Think about your circle of friends. One of them might be looking for the same kind of mutual encouragement. Look for someone who has a positive, can-do attitude, who is as committed to their goals as you are to yours, someone reliable and comfortable with giving you candid feedback and vice versa. Regularly update each other on your progress, challenges, and wins. Checking in with a friend or colleague gives you some social pressure to follow through, and they can provide encouragement as well. The downside may be that your accountability partner might not have the same level of commitment as you and depending on who you choose as your accountability partner, the person may be more lenient, which reduces the pressure for you to perform.

3. Group Accountability

Join a group focused on a shared goal, like a fitness class or a professional development group. Regular meetings and check-ins are common. Community support gives you strength in numbers and you may receive varied perspectives, including different approaches to the same goal. The downside is the group's size; it is easier to hide in a crowd and you are at the mercy of the group dynamics, with some personalities clashing or differences of opinion getting in the way of personal progress.

4. Professional Accountability

Hire or consult with a professional such as a business coach, consultant, or advisor. Regular meetings and performance reviews are often part of the arrangement. The prime benefit would be receiving expert guidance from a seasoned professional, who can empower you and enhance your effectiveness to achieve significant progress. I once had to make a business decision to replace one of my vendors with one that was more efficient. If it were not for my business coach Deborah Dickerson, I would have never recognized a change needed to be made. Even though I knew in my gut I could do better, without the accountability from my business coach, the changes would have been put on the back burner, because letting a vendor go is uncomfortable. The downside to hiring professional accountability is that you need to set time aside for regular coaching sessions and with so many different coaches available, sometimes it is difficult to tell who you should hire. I would recommend interviewing several coaches prior to choosing one, and asking colleagues, friends, and family for recommendations. If you are looking for a business coach to advise you on basic business principles, you may be able to receive free business coaching and workshops through a Small Business Development Center near you: https://americassbdc.org. I highly recommend also finding a coach who has industry experience in your field, because they know exactly what it's like to be in your shoes and know what it takes to succeed in your industry. They also have a deeper level of insight required to propel you to the top of your industry. For this reason, I have several people who I turn to for business coaching and advice. Having multiple coaches with industry-specific knowledge can offer perspectives and insights tailored to different situations. For example, if you are mapping out the long-term vision for your business, you might consult with a coach within your industry. If you're faced with operational challenges, seek advice from someone who excels in operational management with hands-on experience. When thinking of introducing a new product or service, consult with an expert who has overseen product launches or innovations that can offer critical insights. Each advisor brings a unique set of experiences and knowledge, equipping you to tackle challenges from multiple perspectives.

5. Public Accountability

Declare your goals publicly, for example, on social media. Some people even blog about their progress. The stakes are higher and having that social pressure can be a powerful motivator. The downside, however, can be that public failure can be humiliating.

One form of public accountability I recently set up was collecting Google reviews. Collecting reviews can build trust and credibility and act as proof, giving potential customers, your referral partners, and even potential future prospective employees confidence in your products or services. Google reviews also play a significant role in local search ranking (when someone searches for your services on Google, your business is more visible when you rank higher). Collecting reviews from clients will also give you valuable feedback and insight into what you are doing right and where improvements are needed to better serve your customers. With focus, you can collect reviews over time that will add up quickly. My team and I were able to collect over one hundred five-star reviews within a nine-month frame, with the majority of those reviews coming in the last quarter of the year.

Here are the steps to setting up your Google business listing and collecting reviews:

Setting Up Google Reviews:

✧ **Create or Claim Your Google My Business Listing:** If you haven't already, create a Google My Business (GMB) listing. If your business is already listed, claim it.

✧ **Complete Your Profile:** Fill in all relevant details such as business name, address, phone number, and operating hours.

✧ **Verify Your Business:** Google will send a verification code through mail, email, or phone. Enter the code to verify your listing.

✧ **Get Your Review Link:** Once verified, navigate to the "Get More Reviews" section in your GMB dashboard and copy the shareable link.

Collecting Reviews:

✧ **Ask Directly:** The most straightforward way to get a review is to ask satisfied customers directly.

✧ **Use Automation:** My friend Jacquie Walter inspired me to use automation to collect Google Reviews. My sister Helen and her husband Jon, both software engineers, set up my automation for me, but you can hire someone to do this part. If your Customer Relationship Management (CRM) software has the capability, set up workflows. For example, when an individual's status changes from "Prospect" to "Client" an email is automatically sent to them with the link to ask for a review.

✧ **Website and Social Media:** Promote your Google review link on your website and through social media channels.

✧ **In-Store Promotions:** If you have a physical location, use signage to encourage reviews.

Dos and Don'ts

Dos:

✧ **Ask at the Right Time:** Request reviews when the customer has just had a positive experience.

✧ **Make It Easy:** Use QR codes or direct links to guide people to the review page.

✧ **Say Thank You:** Always acknowledge customers for their reviews, whether positive or negative.

✧ **Be Professional:** If you receive a negative review, reply professionally, and address any issues.

Don'ts:

✧ **Don't Pay for Reviews:** Paid reviews are against Google's policies and can get your business penalized.

✧ **Don't Ask for Reviews in Bulk:** Sending mass requests

can appear spammy, insincere, and you will end up with a bunch of missing reviews. If you suspect there are missing reviews, you can report it to Google. I had several clients send me screenshots of their submitted reviews that never showed up. After reporting this to Google, twelve of the missing reviews popped up on our business profile within a few days. I shared this tip with a friend who had been suspicious of missing reviews, and fifteen missing reviews showed up after she inquired! Visit this site: https://support.google.com/business/gethelp.

✧ Log into your account, type in "missing reviews" and follow the prompts. It will help if you can give examples of clients who have submitted reviews that never showed up.

✧ **Don't Ignore Negative Reviews:** Always respond to negative reviews. Ignoring these can damage your brand image and sometimes how you respond to negative feedback can help gain confidence in your commitment to the service you provide.

✧ **Don't Use Fake Reviews:** This could result in your business listing being suspended.

Incorporating technology into your accountability strategy can provide an effective approach to staying on track. Here are a few ways you can leverage technology for accountability; many of these tools have free and upgraded versions:

Task Management Apps

Examples: Todoist, Asana, Trello

✧ **How It Works:** Create tasks, set deadlines, and prioritize.

✧ **Benefits:** Real-time syncing, notification reminders, and collaboration features.

Habit-Tracking Apps

Examples: Habitica (Gamify Your Life!), Streaks

- ✧ **How It Works:** Log daily habits and strive for consistency.

- ✧ **Benefits:** Gamification elements can make habit formation more engaging.

Screen Time and Website Blockers

- ✧ **Examples:** Freedom (freedom.to), Cold Turkey

- ✧ **How It Works:** Block distracting websites or set screen time limits.

- ✧ **Benefits:** Forces focus by removing distractions.

Understanding the different types of accountability implementing tools can set the stage for more successful outcomes in your endeavors. My conversations, like the one with Katie about my book, and the professional experiences I had under Vince's leadership, underscore the profound impact of having systems of accountability in place. It's easy to lose sight of our goals amidst life's distractions, but having someone to answer to keeps us grounded and propels us ahead. As you finish this chapter, I urge you to reflect on your "whys" and intertwine them with layers of accountability. For when we align our passion with responsibility, we find ourselves on a course not just towards success but towards fulfillment.

Chapter 12 Smart Moves

1. Reflect on ways you will reward yourself for achieving short-term goals and evaluate your "whys," which ties into your consequences.

2. Evaluate, identify, and implement at least three types of accountability processes.

3. Set up your Google profile (if you haven't already) and start collecting Google reviews from clients.

A Closing Perspective: The Magnetic Pull

Navigating the landscape of human connection is an art, as intricate and subtle as it is powerful. In this book, spanning twelve chapters, I hope to have helped you embark on the journey of cultivating an innate magnetism within yourself. This whole journey, if you remember, began with one goal in mind: helping you build referral partners to seriously amp up your business game.

And it's not just about business cards and LinkedIn connections. Whether we're discussing how to master the art of becoming that fascinating person others are drawn to, recognizing talent in others, or making your mark and shining in the digital realm, it's all tied back to creating that magnetic appeal. The kind that gets people talking about you, referring you, and wanting to work with you. To create genuine, lasting connections. All these chapters, all these lessons, they loop back to one thing: making you a referral magnet.

In closing, I want you to consider this: every material—wood, plastic, even water—will respond to a magnetic field if it's strong enough. Now imagine how much more a human being, with all our complexities and emotions, can respond to your magnetic appeal. When I first started putting this book together, I was thinking of qualities of a magnetic person, metaphorically . . . then later, I found research that shows that the human heart produces electromagnetic fields that can be measured up to three feet from your body! I looked into it further. I was curious what the correlation and differences were between electromagnetic versus magnetic. Electromagnetic can be temporarily magnetic, versus magnetic, which is permanent. I found this to be validating . . . that people can be legitimately physically magnetic.

As you implement these principles, remember that if at first you don't see the magnetism, if you're putting in the work and the referrals are not flooding in just yet, don't be discouraged. Keep at it, lean into all the lessons we've explored, do more to create a stronger magnetic attraction. Here's to you attracting not just any connections, but the meaningful, golden ones that open doors to endless opportunities. Cheers to a future filled with magnetic moments and prosperous partnerships!

Appendix A
Top Careers That Rely on Referrals and Power Referral Partners' Ideas

Attorneys:

- ✧ **Accountants:** They may work with clients who have complex financial matters requiring legal expertise.

- ✧ **Real estate agents:** They often encounter clients who need legal assistance with property transactions or disputes.

- ✧ **Other attorneys:** Referrals can come from attorneys specializing in different areas of law or seeking co-counsel for cases.

Car Salespersons:

- ✧ **Auto mechanics:** They may refer clients who are in the market for a new or used car to the salesperson for assistance with vehicle selection and purchase.

- ✧ **Insurance agents:** They may refer clients who need to purchase a vehicle and require insurance coverage for their new vehicle.

- ✧ **Real estate agents:** They may refer clients who are relocating or in need of a new vehicle to accommodate their lifestyle or work needs.

Consultants:

⬦ **Industry experts:** They may refer clients who need specialized consulting services outside of their own expertise.

⬦ **Former clients:** Satisfied clients may refer others in their network who could benefit from consulting services.

⬦ **Business coaches:** They often work with clients on personal and professional development and may recommend consulting services to address specific business challenges.

Event Planners:

⬦ **Caterers:** They often work with event planners to coordinate food and beverage services for events and special occasions.

⬦ **Photographers:** They may refer clients who need event planning services to coordinate logistics and manage event details for weddings, parties, or corporate events.

⬦ **Venue managers:** They may refer clients who need event planning services to find suitable venues for their events and coordinate event logistics and services.

Financial Advisors:

⬦ **Accountants:** They assist clients with tax planning and financial management, complementing the services of financial advisors.

⬦ **Attorneys:** They handle legal matters related to estate planning, business law, and other areas that intersect with financial planning.

⬦ **Insurance agents:** They provide insurance products that align with clients' financial goals and risk management needs.

Freelance Creative Professionals (e.g., graphic designers, writers, photographers):

◆ **Marketing agencies:** They may need specialized creative services for client projects or campaigns.

◆ **Web developers:** They often collaborate with creative professionals to design and develop websites and digital content.

◆ **Small business owners:** They may require various creative services for branding, marketing materials, or content creation.

Home Inspectors:

◆ **Real estate agents:** They often refer clients who need home inspections as part of the home buying process.

◆ **Property managers:** They may refer clients who need property assessments for rental properties or investment properties.

◆ **Insurance agents:** They may refer clients who need home inspections for insurance purposes or to assess property risks.

Insurance Agents:

◆ **Realtors:** They often work with clients who need homeowners' insurance when purchasing a property.

◆ **Financial planners:** They help clients with long-term financial planning, including risk management, through insurance products.

◆ **HR professionals:** They may refer employees or clients who need various insurance products such as health, life, or disability insurance.

IT Consultants:

✧ **Software developers:** They may refer clients who need IT consulting services to address technical challenges or enhance software solutions.

✧ **System administrators:** IT professionals responsible for managing computer systems and networks may refer clients who need consulting services for infrastructure upgrades or security enhancements.

✧ **Tech bloggers:** Influential individuals or organizations in the tech industry may refer clients to IT consultants based on their expertise and track record of success.

Interior Designers:

✧ **Realtors:** They often refer clients who need interior design services to stage properties for sale or enhance the visual appeal of homes.

✧ **Architects:** They may refer clients who need interior design services to complement architectural plans or design concepts for renovation projects.

✧ **Furniture retailers:** They may refer clients who need interior design services to coordinate furniture selections and design aesthetics for residential or commercial spaces.

Marketing Consultants:

✧ **Web designers:** They may refer clients who need marketing services to enhance their online presence or digital marketing strategies.

✧ **Business coaches:** They often work with clients on overall business growth and development and may recommend marketing services to improve branding or customer outreach.

✧ **Industry influencers:** Individuals or organizations with influence in specific industries may refer clients to marketing consultants based on their expertise and track record of success.

Massage Therapists:

✧ **Chiropractors:** They often work with clients who can benefit from massage therapy to complement their chiropractic treatments.

✧ **Physical therapists:** They may refer clients who need massage therapy to address muscle tension, pain, or mobility issues.

✧ **Fitness instructors:** They may refer clients who need massage therapy to alleviate muscle soreness, improve flexibility, or enhance recovery after workouts.

Medical Professionals (e.g., doctors, dentists, physical therapists):

✧ **Specialists:** Doctors or healthcare professionals with specialized expertise may refer patients to other specialists for specific medical conditions or treatments.

✧ **Medical associations:** Organizations or networks within the medical community may refer patients or provide resources for medical professionals.

✧ **Patients:** Satisfied patients may refer others to their healthcare providers based on their positive experiences and outcomes.

Mortgage Brokers:

✧ **Real estate agents:** They often refer clients who need mortgage financing to purchase properties.

✧ **Financial advisors:** They may refer clients who need assistance with mortgage financing as part of their overall financial plan.

✧ **Home builders:** They may refer clients who need mortgage financing to finance new home construction or renovation projects.

Personal Trainers:

✧ **Nutritionists:** They may refer clients who need personal training services to complement their nutrition and wellness goals.

✧ **Physical therapists:** They may refer clients who need personalized exercise programs or rehabilitation services to improve mobility, strength, and overall fitness.

✧ **Gym owners:** They may refer clients who need personal training services to achieve their fitness goals and maximize their gym membership experience.

Real Estate Agents:

✧ **Mortgage brokers:** They often work closely with real estate agents to help clients secure financing for home purchases.

✧ **Home inspectors:** They inspect properties for potential issues, making them crucial for home buying transactions.

✧ **Property managers:** They handle rental properties, and referrals from real estate agents can lead to new clients or property listings.

Recruiters:

✧ **HR professionals:** They may refer companies or colleagues who are seeking recruitment services for staffing needs.

✧ **Industry insiders:** Contacts within specific industries may refer job opportunities or candidates to recruiters.

✧ **Job seekers:** Satisfied candidates may refer others to the recruiter based on their positive experience and successful placement.

Travel Agents:

✧ **Hotel managers:** They often work with travel agents to book accommodations for clients traveling for leisure or business.

✧ **Tour operators:** Travel agents collaborate with tour operators to organize guided tours, excursions, or vacation packages for clients.

✧ **Destination experts:** Local experts or tourism boards provide valuable insights and recommendations to travel agents for planning trips to specific destinations.

Wedding Planners:

✧ **Venues:** Hotels, banquet halls, resorts, and event spaces often refer couples to wedding planners, especially those who book their venue for their wedding.

✧ **Photographers and videographers:** Wedding photographers and videographers frequently refer clients to wedding planners to ensure smooth coordination of the wedding day, allowing them to focus on capturing special moments.

✧ **Florists and decorators:** Florists and decorators collaborate with wedding planners to bring the couple's vision to life, creating cohesive design concepts and ensuring seamless setup and breakdown of décor elements.

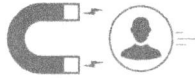

Bibliography

"About Us." America's SBDC, October 20, 2023. https://americassbdc.org/about-us/.

Allen, Erik. Erik Allen Media. https://erikallenmedia.com/resources-podcasting

Baer, Jay. "Why Content is Fire and Social Media is Gasoline." Convince & Connect. https://www.convinceandconvert.com/content-marketing/why-content-is-fire-and-social- media-is-gasoline/.

Breault, Robert. *"Charisma is not so much getting people to like you as getting people to like themselves when you're around."* Professor, University of Utah School of Music. https://music.utah.edu/faculty/robert-breault.php.

Brindle, Christian. "Medicare & ACA Success With Malia Rogers! (Seven Figures Or Bust, Ep 16)." YouTube. https://www.youtube.com/watch?v=k5s4MIbqMrE.

Buffett, Warren. *"It takes twenty years to build a reputation and five minutes to ruin it."* Chairman and CEO, Berkshire Hathaway. https://www.berkshire-hathaway.com/.

Burt, Micheal. "Activate Your Prey Drive, Unleash Your Potential." Coach Micheal Burt. https://www.coachburt.com/.

Busch, May. "What Makes a Person Interesting?" May Busch Creating Leaders. https://maybusch.com/what-makes-person-interesting/.

Carnegie, Dale. *"There are four ways, and only four ways, in which we have contact with the world. We are evaluated and classified by these four contacts: what we do, how we look, what we say, and how we say it."* Motivational speaker. https://www.dalecarnegie.com/en/approach/heritage.

Chase, Emma. *Tamed*. New York: Simon & Schuster, 2014.

Day, Robin. "Just Ask: The Power Of Referrals." *Forbes*. https://www.forbes.com/sites/forbesbusinesscouncil/2021/12/02/just-ask-the-power-of referrals/?sh=3200db537f0d

De Witt Van Amburgh, Fred. "Gratitude is a currency that we can mint for ourselves and spend without fear of bankruptcy." Publisher and author.

Dickerson, Deborah. North Idaho Small Business Development Center. https://idahosbdc.org/locations/north-idaho/.

Dillon, Melissa. The Insurance Exam Queen. https://www.insuranceexamqueen.com

Doby, Danielle. *I Am Her Tribe*. Kansas City, Mo.:⊠ Andrews McMeel Publishing, 2018.

Erickson, Heather. Heather Erickson Studios. https://www.facebook.com/HeatherEricksonStudios/.

Geyser, Werner. "What is Referral Marketing and How Marketers Succeed by Tapping Into It?" Influencer Marketing Hub. https://influencermarketinghub.com/what-is-referral-marketing/.

Hagy, Jessica. *How to Be Interesting (In 10 Simple Steps)*. New York: Workman Publishing Company, 2013.

Hamilton, Josh. Your Retirement Coach. https://www.facebook.com/groups/yourretirementcoach/.

Hurst, Greg. "Memphis company chooses ministry over millions, shares profits with community." WREG-TV, Memphis. https://wreg.com/news/memphis-company-chooses- ministry-over-millions-shares-profits-with-community/.

Jackson, Louise. "10 signs you have an interesting personality and people love spending time with you." Hack Spirit. https://hackspirit.com/signs-you-have-an-interesting-personality/.

Generous Giving. "Journey of Generosity." Founded in 2000 by The Maclellan Foundation. https://generousgiving.org/events/jog/.

Kalu, Ndukwe Kalu. *"The things you do for yourself are gone when you are gone, but the things you do for others remain as your legacy."* A Nigerian-born political scientist at Auburn University, Montgomery. https://www.aum.edu/directory/kalu-kalu/.

Lima, Jamie Kern. "2023 America's Self-Made Women Net Worth." *Forbes.* https://www.forbes.com/profile/jamie-kern-lima/?sh=6a5163f066c1.

Love, Roger. "How To Improve Your Speaking Voice." https://rogerlove.com/speaking/.

Mackay, Harvey.*"Most fears of rejection rest on the desire for approval from other people.*
Don't base your self-esteem on their opinions." Author and business speaker. https://harveymackay.com/about/.

Maslow, A. H. "A theory of human motivation." *Psychological Review 50*:4 (1943), 370-96.

McCormick, Michael. Insurance Soup™. https://www.facebook.com/THEInsuranceSoup.

Mehrabian, Albert, and Ferris, Susan. "Inference of Attitudes from Nonverbal Communication in Two Channels." *Journal of Consulting Psychology* 31:3 (1967), 248-252.

Morales, Jessica I. "The Heart's Electromagnetic Field Is Your Superpower." *Psychology Today.* https://www.psychologytoday.com/us/blog/building-the-habit-of-hero/202011/the-hearts- electromagnetic-field-is-your-superpower.

Mylett, Ed. *The Power of One More: The Ultimate Guide to Happiness and Success.* Hoboken, NJ: Wiley, 2022.

Nemko, Marty. "The Talk Rule." *Psychology Today.* https://www.psychologytoday.com/us/blog/how-do-life/201911/

the-talk-rule#:~:text=Those%20benefits%20and%20liabilities%20 form,conversation%2C%2010%20to%2020%20percent.

Porter, Cheryl. "Learn to Sing." Cheryl Porter Vocal Method. https://cheryl-portermethod.com/.

Proctor, Bob. *"Accountability is the glue that ties commitment to the result."* Canadian author, partner, Proctor Gallagher. https://www.proctorgallagh-erinstitute.com/our-story.

Robbins, Mel. *The 5 Second Rule: Transform Your Life, Work, and Confidence with Everyday Courage.* New York: Savio Republic, 2017.

Rohn, Jim. *"You are the average the average of the five people you spend the most time with."* Motivational speaker. https://www.jimrohn.com/jim-rohn-biography/.

Rosenthal, Robert, and Jacobson, Lenore. *Pygmalion in the Classroom: Teacher Expectation and Student Intellectual Development.* New York: Holt, Rinehart & Winston, 1968.

Schluter, Adam. "What is Monday Night Dinner?" *Hello from A Stranger.* https://www.hellofromastranger.com/monday-night-dinner.

Scott, Elizabeth. "Hedonic Adaptation: Why You Are Not Happier." *Verywell Mind.* https://www.verywellmind.com/hedonic-adaptation- 4156926#:~:tex-t=The%20hedonic%20treadmill%2C%20also%20known,of%20happiness%20 we%20experienced%20prior.

Sing Sharp. "Learn to Sing" mobile app. https://www.singsharp.com/.

Van Edwards, Vanessa. *Cues: Master the Secret Language of Charismatic Com-munication.* London: Penguin Publishing Group, 2022.

Zippia. "How Many Ads Does a Person See in a Day?"

https://www.zippia.com/answers/how-many-ads-does-a-person-see-in-a-day/.

Acknowledgements

Jesus, my Lord and savior, who's plans for us are always greater than what we ever dream of, for shielding me from harm's way and for saving my life (probably more times than I'll ever know). My husband Chris, who inspires the many lives that he touches, has a killer sense of humor and has been a great supporter through my journey. Thank you for your grace and for picking up the slack when I fall short.

My girls Reaghan and Avalyn, who bring me so much joy and one of my biggest "whys," when I am pushing through tough seasons.

My incredible team, Susan Fulton and Martina Meinke-Tyler, who always have my back, who have taken heavy burdens off my shoulders and without you both, I would never have had the opportunity to write this book.

My Beta readers, who were super encouraging, helped me clarify my thoughts and understood my vision for my book: Nancy Brumfield, Gary Murfin, Clarissa Wilson, Scott Bull, Tena Crosby.

My friends and family, who were supportive and cheered me on during this long book writing process. I didn't tell many people during the writing process, so if I told you…you were one of the few people that knew.

Real people in my life that inspired me enough to include in my book:

Adam Schluter, Andrew Strange, Anh Nguyen (my mom), Becky Rill, Christian Brindle, Christopher Rogers (my husband), Courtney Allen, David Clinton, Dean Wong, Deborah Dickerson, Erik Allen, Gary Murfin, Gaylan Hendricks, Heather Erickson, Helen Crowell, Jacquie Walter, Jason Hamilton, Jon Crowell, Katie Salie, Keith Boe, Laura Wong, Martina Meinke-Tyler, Melissa Dillon, Michael McCormick, Micheal Burt, Nancy Brumfield, Robyn Clinton, Taylor Dobbie, Teresa Ferrin, Vincent McPhail

Book writing coach: Debra Englander
Editors: Rachel Shuster, Valerie Costa, Steve Scholl
Production: Cristina Smith
Book Cover and Interior Design: Christy Day
Logo & Workbook Design: Shannon Siriani (Ink Art Design)
Headshots: Tami Siriani (Siriani Photography)
Website: Zach Spain (ZS Design)

Luminary Recommendations

Malia Rogers hit a home run with her book, **Magnetic Allure.** *She has combined the values of verbal and non-verbal communication, the attributes of being a good person and friend, and how a heart full of generosity and genuine character can lead you to success in business and life. I have never seen this much essential content piled into one book.*

–J. Scott Bull
Former NFL Quarterback, San Francisco 49ers
Former CEO Pace Industries Inc.

Malia Rogers' book on networking, **Magnetic Allure** *is a game-changer. This book is a must-read for anyone seeking to elevate their networking skills. With Malia's expert guidance, readers will unlock the secrets to cultivating their own "it" factor, forging meaningful connections, and harnessing the power of magnetic allure to attract valuable leads. Whether you're a seasoned business owner, a dynamic salesperson, or someone who thrives on referrals, Malia's invaluable insights will propel you to new heights of success. Personally mentored by Malia, I can attest to the transformative impact of her teachings. Thanks to her mentorship, I've catapulted my health insurance brokerage into a thriving, six-figure enterprise—and the momentum continues to build. Dive into Malia's book and prepare to revolutionize your approach to networking and professional growth.*

–Jacquie Walter
Founder, Translating Insurance LLC

Living in a sea of busy people and new ideas every day, it can often be challenging to build a meaningful community of friends and business associates. Malia expertly outlines a series of essential skills to become a magnetic person who will enrich—and be enriched- by those around you. The tools found here can help guide business professionals, or anyone looking for meaningful community, to a life filled with genuine and lasting relationships.

–Clarissa Wilson
Co-Designer of Award-Winning Board Game, Everdell
Entrepreneur and Mom of Seven Wonderful Kids

Malia's book breaks down a simple strategy to grow a business PLUS the energy to be magnetic, now anyone can grow and sustain an incredible business! Having built a multi-million-dollar business selling exam prep material, I know the power of making personal connections and harnessing powerful networks. Malia teaches people how to tap into their own personal power so they can stand out in the crowd and fully utilize networks for their businesses. Anyone reading this book is doing themselves a huge favor! Thank you so much Malia for offering such incredible wisdom to the world!

–Melissa Dillon
5 Star Backed Insurance Exam Queen
YouTube Influencer & Entrepreneur

Malia Rogers is one of those rare individuals who leaves an everlasting impact on everyone she meets. An effortless high achiever of the highest character, she has the ability to light up any room or turn the most mundane business meeting into a bright, friendly and memorable adventure. She truly has the 'Midas Touch'; any pursuit turns to gold under Malia's guidance. Everyone who knows her instantly picks up on her pure, permeating 'Magnetic Allure'. Her enthusiasm is contagious, and you'll find it on every page of this book, inspiring you with every word.

–Keith Boe
Founder of North Idaho Life
Lifelong Entrepreneur, Business Marketeer & Strategist
Voted Best Real Estate Agent in North Idaho 2018-2024